Design

Of the 59 battleships commissioned by the US Navy 55 followed the same design principle: heavy armament and protection at the expense of speed. The last four, the *Iowa* class, did not; they were very fast. They also had the longest and most active service life of any class of battleship. The *Iowa*s were also well armed and well protected, but no more so than their immediate predecessors, the *South Dakota* class.

Like all battleships built just prior to the Second World War, these classes had their genesis in the Washington Naval Treaty. In 1922 all the major naval powers signed this treaty that was intended to stop competitive naval building programs where each great power tried to outbuild the others with more and larger ships of each category. The treaty limited the number of battleships and total naval tonnage that each country could build, and also set a maximum tonnage for new battleships. Furthermore, a battleship 'holiday' was declared – no new battleships could be built until the 1930s.

Therefore, when it came to replacing the oldest battleships in the US Navy, the General Board had plenty of time to decide what was important for the next generation of battleships. The following issues were considered – armament, speed and protection. With regard to armament the General Board of Construction favoured the 16in gun, which it had used successfully in the *Maryland* class built in the early 1920s. However, the London Treaty of 1930 limited displacement to 35,000 tons and 14in weapons. Their first designs (which were to become the *North Carolina* class) were for a ship armed with twelve 14in guns (in quadruple turrets) and protection against 14in gunfire. The speed was set at 27kts – 6kts faster than the *Maryland* class but slower than most of the other battleships building abroad. The speed of 27kts was decided upon to counter the Japanese battlecruisers of the *Kongo* class, which were thought to have a speed of 26.5kts. Actually the *Kongo*s had been rebuilt and were now classed as battleships but could achieve 30kts. At the last moment, the General Board took advantage of a get-out clause in the London treaty and upgraded the armament to nine 16in guns in three triple turrets. It was too late to increase the protection so the *North Carolina*s were a bit under-protected considering their armament. The secondary armament consisted of twenty 5in 38-calibre dual-purpose weapons in ten twin housings. The dual-purpose armament was an advanced concept and recognised the importance of anti-aircraft armament.

The *North Carolina* class was succeeded by the *South Dakota* class. The protection was upgraded to be able to withstand 16in gunfire while keeping the same armament, speed and displacement. This was achieved by some design compromises, notably a reduction in hull length so as to reduce the extent of the armour belt. The result was a solid but somewhat cramped ship with reasonable speed, good protection and heavy armament.

The *Iowa* class were a response to the need for a fast battleship to keep up with the new aircraft carriers and to be able to cope with rumoured new Japanese 'super-cruisers'. These design requirements were intended to produce a special type that could be put into service without too much delay or deviation. The next design – the

A view of the *New Jersey* as first commissioned in 1943. One can see the purposeful lines, the two graceful and well-proportioned funnels, and the long sweeping bow that distinguished this class from its predecessors.

■ SHIP STATISTICS

Dimensions		Propulsion	
Length overall	887ft 3in	Boilers	eight Babcox and Wilcox
At waterline	860ft	Engines	four geared turbines
Beam	108ft 2in	Output	212,000shp
Draft	36ft 2in	Speed	32.75kts
Height above water		Endurance	15,000nm @ 15kts
Bow	36ft		
Stern	22ft	Protection	
Bridge	65ft	Belt armour	12.1in STS
Stack	98ft	Deck armour	6.75in
Mast	34ft	Turret face	18.75in
Tonnage standard	46,062	Side	10.25in
Full load	57,322 (1944)	Conning tower	17in

The raison d'etre of the *Iowa* class – high speed and 16in 50-calibre guns.

Montana class – was to be the definitive battleship. To achieve the General Board's requirements, the *South Dakota* design was the starting point, but lengthened by 200ft and displacement increased by 10,000 tons to accommodate the extra machinery and provide a hull shape to achieve a 6kt increase in speed.

The General Board of Naval Construction considered the *Iowa* class an aberration with a specific mission and immediately went back to designing the type of battleship they really liked: powerfully armed, well protected and not too fast. Had this design ever been completed as the *Montana* class, it is hard to imagine them having as long and as successful careers as the *Iowa*s. In fact this 'aberration' is considered one of the best battleship designs ever.

The 16in 50-calibre weapon was chosen over several other alternatives. The 16in/45 used in the *South Dakota*s and *North Carolina*s was considered but abandoned because it was felt that for the extra tonnage and expenditure some increase in firepower was required. Even 18in guns were investigated – they offered a better range and heavier projectile but they were very heavy, so only six could be mounted in place of nine 16in guns. A 16in 56-calibre weapon was also in the running but although it offered a better range the barrel wear and rate of fire would be inferior. As far as range was concerned, these weapons were already firing over the horizon anyway and a greater range was useless unless

there was fire control to match. The 16in/50 was considered a perfect balance, since it fired a heavier projectile than the 16in/45s at an equivalent rate and with more accuracy. The secondary armament of twenty 5in 38-calibre remained the same as the previous classes but it was located a deck higher than the *North Carolina*s and had better arcs of fire than the *South Dakota*s. As already pointed out, the 5in/38 was a dual-purpose weapon – used for surface action and against aircraft.

Initially there were plans for 1.1in quads and .50-calibre machine guns for AA protection but these were abandoned for the more powerful 40m quads and 20mm cannons. As time went on the AA armament was increased considerably.

The 50-calibre 16in gun was a formidable weapon capable of firing a 2700lb projectile a distance of 39,800yds (22.6 miles). These guns could fire at a rate of slightly over two rounds a minute. The main armament was mounted in a slightly larger turret that was better armoured than the ones used in the previous classes. It also compared well with its likely adversary, the *Yamato* class's 18in guns. The projectile was 18 per cent lighter but it could be fired faster and with better accuracy.

These guns were guided by two Mk 38 directors mounted on the top of the bridge on the fire control platform and atop the aft fire control tower forward of Turret 3. The rangefinder of this gun director measured 26.5ft.

The secondary armament of 5in/38 dual-purpose guns was similar to previous classes. Due to the relative shortness of the barrel, it sacrificed accuracy and range for ease of handling and rapidity of fire. A trained crew could fire 14 rounds a minute. It could be elevated at angles up to 85 degrees and fire a 54lb shell as high as 27,000ft.

The *New Jersey* was reactivated in 1968 as a gunfire support ship for the Vietnam conflict. All of her light AA armament was removed and she relied upon electronic means to defend herself from airborne attack – both from aircraft and guided missiles. A ULQ-6B electronic jammer was mounted atop the foremast.

In the 1980s this class was reactivated and given a comprehensive weapons upgrade. The key features of this class, the propulsion and main armament, were kept intact as they had stood the test of time.

Tomahawk missiles were put in armoured box launchers to protect them from the blast of the 16in guns. They are formidable weapons with a range of 1500 miles for land attack and 300 miles for the anti-ship version. This weapon is very accurate – it is expected to land within 10 metres of the target.

Harpoon missiles are a surface-skimming anti-ship missile carrying a 570lb warhead. The launchers are mounted on each side of the after funnel.

■ MAIN ARMAMENT STATISTICS

16in 50-calibre gun Mk 7

Length	68ft	Maximum range	40,000yds
Weight	120 tons	Rate of fire	2.1rpm
Muzzle velocity	2600 f/s	Projectile weight	2700lb

■ ARMAMENT

Main armament	9 x 16in 50-calibre
Secondary armament	20 x 5in 38-calibre

Light anti-aircraft armament

	As Commissioned		1945		1950	
	20mm	40mm in quads	20mm	40 in quads	20mm in twins	40mm in quads
Iowa	60	60	52	76	0	60**
New Jersey	57	64	49	80	32*	64**
Missouri	49	80	49	80	64*	64**
Wisconsin	49	80	49	80	32*	64**

*Removed by 1953

** 4 quads added when reactivated for Korean War

Armament: 1968 *New Jersey*

Main armament	9 x 16in 50-calibre
Secondary armament	20 x 5in 38-calibre
Anti-aircraft	4 Zuni chaff launchers

Armament: 1985 After modernisation

Main armament	9 x 16in 50-calibre
Secondary armament	12 x 5in 38-calibre
Tomahawk SSMs	8 armoured box launchers
Harpoon anti-ship missiles	4 quadruple launchers
Close-in Weapon Systems	4 Phalanx

For defence against incoming missiles the Phalanx CIWS is an impressive weapon that fires 3000 rounds of depleted uranium per minute. When in action it sounds like paper being torn rather than the stutter of a conventional machine gun. It is controlled by a closed loop system, tracking both the target and the projectiles to ensure that the two meet.

A SC-1 Seahawk floatplane on the catapult of an *Iowa* class battleship.

Missouri's aircraft arrangements, as completed in 1944. The Vought OS2U Kingfisher floatplanes were the battleship's standard air complement until replaced by the SC-1 Seahawk in 1945.

This shows the large area of the rudders, but note also the difference between inboard and outboard propellers.

AIRCRAFT

The *Iowa* class battleships carried aircraft used for scouting and target spotting functions. As commissioned this class were equipped with Vought OS2U Kingfisher floatplanes. These were standard for all battleships and cruisers by 1943, but in 1945 these were replaced by the Curtiss SC-1 Seahawk scout plane which had a longer range and better visibility.

Soon after the war floatplanes were considered more of a liability than an asset; they were fragile and had to be flown off prior to action so that they would not be damaged by gun blast. By the Korean War fixed-wing aircraft had been replaced by helicopters in this role. The first helicopters assigned to the *Iowa* class were Sikorsky HO3S-1s, used during the Korean War and afterwards. Some radio-controlled target drones were also carried for AA practice – a propeller and jet versions were available. Helicopters of most types could use the *Iowa*

quarterdeck facility and in photographs a number of different types can be seen on the fantail. In 1985 the Marine Corps CH-53 helicopter was the spotter of choice.

There was no hangar for aircraft as was the case in other US battleships. The aircraft were stowed on and launched by catapults located on the fantail. There was a crane for retrieving the floatplanes. The catapults were removed when helicopters became the scouting option, but the crane remained because it was useful for aircraft handling operations. In the last refit in the 1980s the crane was removed and special helicopter handling facilities were installed with fuelling stations and stowage for three choppers.

PROPULSION SYSTEM

The propulsion system was the largest plant ever put in a warship. There were eight boilers and four geared turbines (one for each shaft). Experience with the *North Carolina*s and *South Dakota*s showed a tendency to vibration at speeds over 25kts, but the problem was solved in the *Iowa*s by using a four-bladed propeller on the outside shafts and a five-bladed propeller on the inside. This cut down on resonance and damped the vibration: above all, these ships were primarily gun platforms and vibration was a major disadvantage.

Steering was through two large rudders mounted just aft of the inboard shafts. This duplication of rudders and shafts made the ship less vulnerable to a lucky hit astern, such as the one that crippled the single-rudder *Bismarck*.

The hull design of the ship and its powerful machinery and large rudder area made these ships not only fast but very manoeuvrable. They handled more like a destroyer than a battleship – in fact their turning radius was smaller than that of a *Fletcher* class destroyer.

Careers

The *Iowa* class were the longest serving battleships of any nation. Their careers ranged from February 1943 when the *Iowa* was commissioned to March 1992 when the *Missouri* was decommissioned for the third and probably final time. All four battleships are still extant and are expected to remain as museum ships. Their long service life was filled with incident – possibly because of their prominent roles and possibly because of their characteristics, namely a battleship that handled like a destroyer.

While on her shakedown cruise the *Iowa* grounded at the entrance to Casco Bay, Maine. It was a tricky passage into the harbour but the *Iowa* had successfully negotiated it five times previously – and she handled so well that perhaps overconfidence played a part. Captain John McCrea's career was on the line, but his previous reputation, and the fact that the President took an interest because McCrea was a former aide, helped save his bacon.

The *Iowa* was repaired and when she was ready for action she was sent to Newfoundland to provide distant cover for convoys. The German battleship *Tirpitz* was making a nuisance of herself bombarding Spitsbergen and threatening convoys to Murmansk, but any chance for an *Iowa–Tirpitz* battle disappeared when the *Tirpitz* was damaged by British midget submarines in a Norwegian fiord. This was the first of several near meetings with enemy super-battleships.

Her next sortie was one of historic significance: she was to carry all of the top brass, including President Franklin Roosevelt and the CNO Admiral King, to the conference with Churchill at Casablanca. She departed Hampton Roads on 14 November 1943 for this highly confidential mission. She steamed at high speed accompanied by two escort carriers and three destroyers. One day out and still far from the combat zones all the VIPs including the President were on deck to watch the *Iowa* practice her extensive AA battery. At this time – possibly to impress the dignitaries – one of the escorting destroyers, the *William D Porter*, conducted a mock torpedo attack at the navy's newest and most powerful battleship. Accidentally a live torpedo was fired

■ CONSTRUCTION DETAILS

No	Ship	Builder (Navy Yard)	Laid down	Launched	Commission	Decommissioned
BB-61	*Iowa*	New York	27.6.1940	27.8.1942	22.2.1943	26.10.1990
BB-62	*New Jersey*	Philadelphia	16.9.1940	7.12.1942	23.5.1943	8.2.1991
BB-63	*Missouri*	New York	6.1.1941	29.1.1944	11.6.1944	31.3.1992
BB-64	*Wisconsin*	Philadelphia	25.1.1941	7.12.1943	16.4.1944	30.1.1991
BB-65	*Illinois*	Philadelphia	6.12.1942	–	–	Cancelled 11.8.1945
BB-66	*Kentucky*	Norfolk	6.12.1942	20.1.1950	-	Hull BU 9.1958

Iowa underway in the Atlantic shortly after commissioning in 1943.

New Jersey carrying out practice firings in November 1943, before her first Pacific deployment.

directly at the *Iowa* at close range. The captain of the *William D Porter*, Lt Cmdr Wilfred Walter, immediately notified the *Iowa* and Captain McCrea showed his best ship-handling skills by ordering full speed and turning directly towards the offending destroyer. The torpedo was successfully avoided and exploded harmlessly – but close enough to jolt the ship. Admiral King was furious – even more so than usual. Not only had the 'Willi D' (as she was called) endangered the President and the navy's newest and most powerful battleship but she did this in front of the Army's top brass. The entire ship was put under arrest and responsible parties sentenced but the President again took a personal interest and requested that no one be punished because of this incident. So what did happen to Lt Cmdr Wilfred Walter, the captain of the ship that fired a live torpedo at the *Iowa* with the president, CNO and Army top brass on board? The record shows that he served in the US Navy for a long time thereafter and retired as a rear admiral.

After the President was delivered safely to Morocco the *Iowa* turned towards the Pacific. In company with her sister *New Jersey*, which had just finished working up, they transited the Panama Canal in January and joined what was to become the Fifth Fleet.

The Pacific war was entering a new phase at this point. In 1942 the opposing fleets had fought to a standstill with heavy losses on each side, and 1943 was relatively quiet while each side tried to rebuild its naval strength. The US was vastly superior

in this respect. By the end of 1943 the US had commissioned seven new fleet carriers, seven light carriers and added eight new battleships. There was plenty more to come. The Japanese were able to muster only two new battleships – although they were the biggest ever built – and one new carrier. In November the rebuilt US Navy, the 'big blue fleet', sailed from Pearl Harbor and attacked the Gilbert Islands This fleet comprised two main sections – the carrier force to which all the modern battleships were appended, and the invasion force which contained a complement of old battleships for bombardment and protection from surface attack. At this stage of the war the modern battleships' primary mission was to protect the offensively powerful but vulnerable aircraft carriers from surface and air attack.

The *Iowa* and *New Jersey*, the two most powerful and speedy battleships, joined the fleet, as part of Task Force 58 in January. They joined the assault on the Marshall Islands and supported the aircraft carriers during their air strikes. Task Force 58 then launched an attack on the inner defences of the Japanese empire. Their target was the primary base of the Japanese fleet – Truk atoll in the Caroline Islands. The *Iowa* and *New Jersey*, accompanied by a couple of heavy cruisers and a light carrier, were sent to penetrate Japanese defences deeper than ever before. They hoped to catch some major Japanese units but the Combined Fleet had retired several weeks earlier, when they had got wind of the attack.

The two battleships and their consorts swept around Truk atoll and flushed out what was left behind. Two destroyers, a light cruiser and some patrol craft tried to escape from what was once known at the 'Japanese Pearl Harbor', but the *Iowa* and *New Jersey* took the auxiliary *Shonan Maru 15* under fire with their secondary armament and the ship was history shortly after. The *Iowa* and *New Orleans* then opened fire on the light cruiser *Katori*, the *Iowa* using her main armament this time, and the cruiser only lasted 11 minutes. The destroyers *Maikaze* and *Nowaki* were scurrying away as fast as they could in the confusion but the *New Jersey* took on the *Maikaze* at 7000yds. The *Maikaze* managed to get off three torpedoes at the *Iowa* but it did not help her cause; she was gone by lunchtime. The lone remaining ship, the *Nowaki*, was heading away at top speed and was nearly out of range by the time the two battleships put on flank speed in a rare battleship chasing destroyer action. The *Nowaki* just managed to get over the horizon, but not before being straddled by salvoes fired at a range of 35,000yds. The *Nowaki* and the two *Iowa*s would meet again at Leyte. This time the *Nowaki* would not escape.

After the *Nowaki*'s lucky escape the battleships broke out their biggest flags and did a complete circumnavigation of Truk atoll. Militarily the expedition yielded minor results but its symbolism was enormous. It was as though the *Yamato* and *Musashi* sailed around Pearl Harbor in plain view and the US could do nothing about it. Also the *Nowaki* had some tales to tell of battleships that were almost as fast as a destroyer.

After this mission the two battleships rejoined Task Force 58 for the more mundane duties of carrier protection and shore bombardment. Things livened up for the two battleships in June 1944 when the Fifth Fleet mounted an amphibious assault on the Mariana Islands. The Marianas were part of the inner defence circle of the Japanese empire, so any assault on these would require nothing less than a sortie of the Combined Fleet.

The landings were covered by Task Force 58 (TF 58), which had seven attack carriers, eight light carriers and seven modern battleships, including the *Iowa* and *New Jersey*. When the Combined Fleet sailed it contained five battleships and three attack carriers supported by six light carriers. It

was smaller and weaker than TF 58 but it had two advantages – its aircraft had a longer range and it could choose its position in the vast Pacific Ocean. Unfortunately, its chosen position was in a nest of US submarines which took out its two largest carriers and alerted TF 58 to the approach of the Combined Fleet.

Admiral Spruance did an interesting thing as the Combined Fleet approached. He detached his seven battleships and some escorting cruisers and destroyers and positioned this force between his carriers and the Combined Fleet. This was done for two reasons: the forward battleship force could act as an anti-aircraft screen for the carriers and it could be used as a surface action group against the Combined Fleet.

Admiral Ozawa, the commander of the Combined Fleet, manoeuvred to stay just out of range of the American carriers while keeping his own carriers in range. He launched strike after strike at the American carriers which were duly shot down by the *Iowa*'s surface action group, carrier planes and finally by the carriers and their escorts. Over 400 aircraft were downed that day, in what became known as the 'Great Marianas Turkey Shoot' and it destroyed Japanese

Iowa with one of the earlier *South Dakota* class battleships, *Indiana* (BB-58), operating in the Pacific in early 1944, the *Iowa* in Measure 32/1B. Note the three single 20mm guns on No 2 turret, an arrangement unique to this ship (the other three of the class had a quad 40mm mounting on a taller platform in this position).

Iowa and *New Jersey* with the *Washington* and *North Carolina* in Majuro Lagoon.

Two views of *New Jersey* in the Pacific, a couple of months after the Battle of the Philippine Sea. At this point the ship has just become Admiral Halsey's Third Fleet flagship, and would shortly take part in the monumental Battle of Leyte Gulf.

naval aviation for the rest of the war. The battleship surface action group was kept in readiness but the wily Ozawa managed to keep his new location secret. Admiral Willis Lee was reluctant to risk a night action with the Japanese forces, so it was not until late in the next day that the Japanese fleet were located, by which time they were at the maximum range for a carrier strike and heading home fast. Once again the *Iowa*s were denied a chance of a surface action against the *Yamato* and *Musashi*. At least this time they were all in the same battle.

After four months of reverting back to their now familiar role as carrier escorts there was another chance for surface action against their equals – the battle of Leyte Gulf. The Fifth Fleet had now become the Third Fleet and was under the command of Admiral William Halsey. Leyte Gulf was, and still is, the largest naval engagement ever fought. It was also the last action where battleships fought battleships in the manner they were designed to. Present at this massive battle were the *Iowa* and *New Jersey*.

The Imperial Japanese Navy was by now severely outnumbered by the US Navy. Furthermore, the Japanese carrier forces were virtually impotent because of the lack of planes and aircrew. They did, however, possess nine powerful battleships including the massive *Yamato* and *Musashi*, although the US had twelve battleships: six older ones with the amphibious ships in Leyte Gulf and six modern ones escorting the carriers of Task Force 38. The Japanese plan was to separate the two forces and concentrate a surface attack on the ships in Leyte Gulf. To do this a decoy force of four virtually plane-less aircraft carriers escorted by two hybrid carrier-battleships (useless as either carriers or battleships) commanded by Admiral Ozawa was sent from Japan to lure TF 38 north and away from the action in Leyte Gulf.

The main Japanese striking force of seven battleships was split into two groups to make a pincer attack on the ships in Leyte Gulf. The Northern Force, which included the *Yamato* and *Musashi*, was to sneak through San Bernardino Strait in the north and attack simultaneously from the north of the gulf. The Southern Force battleships were to attack at night from the south via Surigao Strait. The Northern Force under Admiral Kurita was detected and attacked by a couple of American submarines that accurately reported the position, composition and direction of the force. They also sank the flagship and another heavy cruiser while they were at it. Things got worse for the Japanese when the carrier aircraft of TF 38 found them in the Sibuyan Sea and subjected them to several massive air attacks and sinking the huge *Musashi* – but leaving the remaining four battleships relatively unharmed.

At this point Admiral Halsey designated a force to be formed to guard San

Iowa conducting a shore bombardment.

Bernardino Strait against the surviving ships. This force, designated Task Force 34, included the *Iowa*, *New Jersey* and four other modern battleships. This force was never actually formed because Halsey had finally found the decoy force and was sucked in by Ozawa's ruse. He rushed to the north taking all his battleships with him. The next day TF 38 was in range of the Japanese decoy force and sank all the carriers as well as some destroyers. The battleships did not fire a shot – not even AA fire. The Japanese Southern Force was detected early and summarily dealt with by the six older battleships the night before. While all this was going on, the Northern Force, which still had four battleships, sneaked through San Bernardino Strait and headed south towards Leyte Gulf. There was only a small force of escort carriers between them and the gulf. Their radio messages calling for assistance were heard all the way to Pearl Harbor.

Admiral Halsey was torn between using his fast battleships to run down and destroy what remained of the decoy force or turn around part of his force and try to catch up with the Japanese force now making its way to Leyte gulf. He waited three hours before deciding to detach his battleships and head south to confront Kurita's force. This force proceeded at a fairly leisurely pace and then stopped to refuel the escorting destroyers, losing another two hours. Finally at 17:00 Halsey detached the *Iowa* and *New Jersey* to do what they did best: race ahead of the rest of the force and engage the enemy's battle line. They sped southwards with three light cruisers and eight destroyers but arrived off the entrance to San Bernardino Strait two hours too late. The once-lucky *Nowaki* was straggling and ran afoul of the two big battleships. This time she didn't get away. Perhaps it was as well that the *Iowa* and *New Jersey* did not catch Kurita's force – it outnumbered them 2:1, but there were four more modern US battleships only 90

Above, left: *New Jersey* with an *Essex* class carrier in heavy weather.

Above, right: The crowds watching the surrender ceremony on the deck of the *Missouri*. On the bulkhead is Commodore Perry's 1853 flag with 31 stars.

Wisconsin freshly arrived in the Pacific late in 1944.

minutes away. This was the closest that the *Iowa*s got to engaging enemy battleships, and the 'what ifs' surrounding this action will remain answered to tease all battleship enthusiasts.

Leyte Gulf more or less finished off the Japanese Navy as an effective fighting force. The *Iowa* and *New Jersey* were joined by the *Wisconsin* in late 1944. By now the Third Fleet boasted eight modern battleships, three of them *Iowa* class. They spent the rest of the war escorting the fast carriers, enduring typhoons, (which the *Iowa*s weathered rather well despite their slender shape and narrow bow) and dealing with kamikaze aircraft. The *Missouri* was hit by one but little damage resulted. There were never more than three *Iowa*s with the fleet at any one time, as at least one was always being refitted.

Near the end of the war the *Iowa*, *Wisconsin* and *New Jersey* conducted the first bombardment of the Japanese coast since 1866. With the Japanese Navy virtually wiped out and the kamikaze threat largely spent, battleships could roam up and down the coast bombarding industrial targets.

The *Wisconsin* went into Tokyo Bay on 29 August to land a contingent of marines, and the *Iowa* and *Missouri* followed the next day. The *Missouri* was chosen for the surrender ceremony because she was the US Navy's newest battleship and because *Missouri* was President Truman's home state. What took place on her deck on 2 September 1945 ensured her everlasting fame. The Japanese diplomatic party was taken aboard via small boats and escorted to the surrender table. Above the table on a bulkhead was attached the flag that Commodore Mathew Perry flew when he first visited Tokyo Bay in 1853. The five-star flags of Nimitz and MacArthur fluttered aloft, the decks swarmed with crew, dignitaries and press corps, and all jostled for a position to observe the surrender. Shigemutsu, the Japanese foreign minister, signed, followed by MacArthur and representatives of all the allied nations. The sun broke through the clouds at this moment as allied aircraft flew overhead.

And then – peace. The era of the battleship was said to be over, superseded by the

aircraft carrier and submarine. All battleships in the US Navy were either scrapped or placed in reserve, except for the four newest, the *Iowa* class. Even these were relegated to cadet training cruises and goodwill voyages. Although their fighting qualities were devalued they were still, along with the *Midway* class carriers, the largest capital ships in the world. Even so, they too were slowly consigned to reserve until by June 1949 the *Missouri* was the only battleship in commission.

She was as always newsworthy. On 17 January 1950 under a new captain, William Brown, she was making a calibration run on the acoustical range in Chesapeake Bay near Thimble Shoals. Brown took the conn and, mistaking some spar buoys which warned of the shoal waters for markers on the range, he started accelerating straight towards the shoal water ignoring all advice from his officers. Captain Brown had a reputation for being

both a bit flamboyant and a martinet; he had previously told his exec not to give advice, as his job was to see that the captain's orders were executed. After ignoring the increasingly frantic advice from the navigator (Brown told him that he was 'lost'), the *Missouri* hit the shoal at 12.5kts and her momentum took her a further half mile up the gently sloping shoal. Captain Brown was court-martialled and found guilty; his career was over. The *Missouri* remained very visibly grounded and a laughingstock ('the first time a battleship hit a bar that sailors didn't like') for two weeks until tugs, dredgers and a high tide floated her off on 1 February 1.

The prestige of battleships was at a low and the *Missouri* was being readied for the reserve fleet when the Korean War broke out on 25 June 1950. The *Missouri* was rushed with all haste to the combat zone and arrived just before the Inchon landings took place. The most famous ship was sent

Above, left: Awaiting the surrender party on the deck of the *Missouri*. Note the Navy Band under the 16in guns.

Above, right: The war is over – the massive flypast after the surrender ceremony.

Missouri freshly arrived off of Korea at the start of the war.

to parade on the opposite coast to deflect attention from the build-up near Inchon. Her shore bombardments were extremely effective and she provided an ideal demonstration of the usefulness of the big gun.

As there was no surface opposition to speak of, the *Missouri* and her sisters confined themselves to shore bombardment and escort duties. The *Missouri* was relieved on the gun line by the *New Jersey* in May 1951, which continued in much the same vein as the *Missouri* providing exceptional shore support for the troops. Not only were the 16in guns used for bombardments which land-based artillery could not even hope to match, but night-time illumination was provided by searchlights and rescue operations were carried out by the battleship's helicopters. Being large ships they also had ample medical facilities and were occasionally used as hospital ships for major injuries or illnesses.

The *New Jersey* in turn was replaced by the *Wisconsin*. There was no threat from North Korean or Chinese naval forces but there was the occasional shore battery. The *New Jersey* was hit by a 155mm shell, killing a sailor and causing the only casualty that the *New Jersey* suffered in the four wars she fought. The *Wisconsin* was simi-

larly hit off the coast of North Korea while shooting at a train; in return the steam locomotive was hit by a 16in shell which obliterated it.

The *Iowa* was the next to serve in the Korean War, replacing the *Wisconsin*. Again bombardment was her primary activity, and she demonstrated the economy and efficacy of battleship bombardment. In one instance near the Manchurian border the *Iowa* matched the tonnage of ordinance dropped by a 200-bomber attack, and with far better accuracy.

By the end of 1952 all four *Iowa*s had served off of Korea. After the *Iowa* departed in October 1952 she was replaced by the *Missouri* and *New Jersey*. Again they unleashed their tremendous ordinance on the Chinese and North Koreans with terrifying accuracy and force. Land-based artillery could not neutralise many gun emplacements whereas the 16in shell – ten times heavier than the largest land artillery – could penetrate just about anything.

In July 1953 an uneasy truce settled over the conflict and the battleships were again relegated to peacetime roles. They served as flagships and took midshipmen on training cruises. For a few hours in June 1954 the four *Iowa* class battleships oper-

Wisconsin in the US Navy's largest floating dry dock, AFDB-1, in April 1952 at Guam, after a tour of duty off Korea. This was the first time an *Iowa* class ship had used this floating dock. The elegant but complex lines of the bow are shown to good effect.

ated together as a unit for the first and only time when the four of them took midshipmen to Guantanamo Bay.

For all the routine operations of peacetime there were still some dramatic incidents. In May 1958 in a dense fog off Norfolk the *Wisconsin* collided with the destroyer *Eaton*, which was very badly damaged and had to be towed stern first into the navy yard. The *Wisconsin*'s bow was damaged, and 68ft of the hull forward was cut off and replaced by a section from the hull of the incomplete *Kentucky*. By this time the *Missouri* had been decommissioned and the *New Jersey* was being readied for the reserve fleet. The *Iowa* was deactivated on 24 February 1958 with the *Wisconsin*, the last active battleship in any navy, decommissioned nine days later on 8 March. For the first time since 1895 the US Navy had no active battleships in service.

All but the *Iowa* class ships were either preserved as museum ships (*Texas*, *Alabama*, *Massachusetts* and *South Carolina*) or broken up by 1960. Nobody was sure what to do with the *Iowa*s, so they were kept in mothballs. By 1964, with the Vietnam War hotting up, there were calls for the reactivation of some heavy cruisers and battleships, but this was opposed by the top brass, who were all carrier admirals. By 1967, however, the US was losing about one aircraft a week over Vietnam. Considering the cost in pilots and aircraft, the reactivation of an *Iowa* class battleship (at around $25 million) would pay for itself within a few weeks. That clinched it – the reactivation was approved within a day of the retirement of the aviation-minded CNO Admiral MacDonald.

In May 1968 the *New Jersey* steamed down the Delaware River en route to her new assignment off the coast of Vietnam. She was stripped of all her light AA guns but had an impressive new electronic suite added. She was still capable of speeds over 33kts and was very recognisably an *Iowa* class BB. After some gunnery practice and

working up trials on the west coast and a visit to the Philippines she arrived off the coast of Vietnam to seaward of the Demilitarised Zone (DMZ). Here she resumed her Korean War duties – shore bombardment. She plied her trade north of the DMZ, destroying enemy troop concentrations, gun emplacements and ammunition caches. The 16in shell was very destructive: one HC round could clear enough jungle for a helicopter landing zone 600ft in diameter. The shell craters were 50ft across and 20ft deep.

In April 1969 the *New Jersey* headed stateside for replenishment and exchange of personnel. She received a Navy Unit Commendation for her work on the gun line. In August that year she was being readied for her second tour off Vietnam when an astounding communiqué from the Defense Department was received: the *Iowa* was to be deactivated. The reasons for this given at the time were vague and contradictory. Melvin Laird, Secretary of the Navy, said it was because of the expense, but another reason proffered was that there were no more 16in gun barrel liners. It all made little sense. There was a hint that emerged years later in a Senate debate over

Above: The *New Jersey* off Korea in May 1951. She was flagship of the Seventh Fleet, commanded by Vice Admiral H M Martin. She carried out her first shore bombardment on 20 May, and return fire from a coast defence battery scored a hit on No 1 Turret, inflicting the ship's only casualties of the Korean War (1 killed and 2 wounded).

Below: *Missouri* and *New Jersey* moored together at Yokosuka on 5 April 1953. *New Jersey* was relieving *Missouri* as flagship of Vice Admiral J H Clark, Commander Seventh Fleet, after the ship's tour of duty off Korea. *New Jersey* would carry out her first bombardment of Korean positions a week later.

Above: An informative aerial view *Wisconsin* in January 1956 showing the layout of the ship at this time.

Below: *New Jersey* in the Panama Canal on her way to Vietnam, 4 June 1968.

the reactivation of all the *Iowa*s, when Senator Warner of Virginia was quoted as saying it 'was ordered from the White House that the ship should be deactivated because it was impeding the peace negotiations.' The *New Jersey* went back into mothballs with her sisters, but she had made a point about the effectiveness and economy of battleship gunfire as a way of delivering ordinance.

In the 1970s the *Iowa*s narrowly escaped scrapping, saved mainly by the Marines who had an interest in gunfire support for amphibious operations. However, as the 1980s approached, several things happened – the last gun-armed cruisers were stricken and the Soviet fleet began a dramatic expansion. By 1980 there was nothing larger than a 5in gun that could be used for shore bombardment. Of course air strikes could be used, but they were very expensive and not as accurate. The cost of keeping ahead of the Soviets was becoming prohibitive so suddenly the modernisation and reactivation of four large fast battle-ships seemed like a very good idea.

The *New Jersey* was the first one to be modernised and she was commissioned for the fourth time in December 1982. She immediately commenced a very active life, reporting for duty with the Pacific Fleet and called in at Pearl, Manila, Subic Bay and then worked with the Seventh Fleet in the Gulf of Siam. She was diverted to Central America because of tensions over Nicaragua, and was then ordered to make speed for another hotspot in the Mediterranean – Beirut. She bombarded Syrian AA positions within the city and the Bekaa valley, and it is said that her bombardments killed the senior Syrian general. The *New Jersey* spent 111 days at sea on her first cruise of this commission, but although she remained active for another six years she saw no further action. When she was decommissioned in February 1991, she retired as the most decorated battleship in history. She is now a museum ship at Camden, *New Jersey*.

The *Iowa* was next out of mothballs, taking over from the *New Jersey* in Central America and later joining NATO forces in the Atlantic. Her next deployment was in the Persian Gulf where, along with her sister *Missouri* she escorted Kuwaiti tankers past Iranian warships. In April 1989 She was off the coast of Puerto Rico conducting a firing exercise when Number 2 turret exploded, blowing the barrel of the middle gun away and killing all 47 crewmen inside the turret. Several investigations were launched, the first concluding that it was

deliberate sabotage by one of the crewmen inside the turret – a sort of spectacular suicide because of a homosexual relationship with another sailor gone wrong. A second investigation, which was perhaps more scientific, decided that the cause was accidental over-ramming in the middle gun. The truth of the matter was as Captain Moosally said: 'Only God knows what really happened in that turret. We're never really going to know for sure.' Largely as a result of the explosion, the *Iowa* retired from service in 1990. The ship is due to open as a museum in July 2012 at San Pedro, the port of Los Angeles.

The *Missouri* was the next one to return to service in 1986 and her first mission was a round the world cruise, the first undertaken by a US battleship since the Great White Fleet of 1908. She then went with the *New Jersey* to the Persian Gulf. A return trip to the Persian Gulf in 1991, however, would be in entirely different circumstances. The *Missouri* arrived in the Gulf in January 1991, six months after Iraq invaded Kuwait. On 17 January 1991 the *Missouri* fired the first shot of Operation Desert Storm when she launched a Tomahawk cruise missile into Iraq. Later that month the *Missouri* moved to the

Above: *New Jersey* in June 1969, two months after her last bombardment off Vietnam. During the conflict her ammunition expenditure almost matched that of both the Second World War and Korea.

Below: *New Jersey* on the gun line near the DMZ towards the end of her final deployment in spring 1969.

Above, left: The Number 2 Turret on the *Iowa* on 19 April 1989. The cause of this explosion has never been definitively determined.

Above, right: *New Jersey* at sea during the first cruise of her fourth commission.

Below: *Missouri* in the Persian Gulf in April 1991 just after the Gulf War ceasefire, at the end of her 48-year career. Note the large radomes on the stack and fire control tower. Note also the 20mm gun tub still on the tip of the bow.

northern end of the Persian Gulf and opened fire against Iraqi positions in Kuwait with her 16in guns, the first time they had been fired in anger in 38 years. When Iraqi forces invaded Saudi Arabia near the town of Khafji on 11 February, the *Missouri* fired her 16in guns in support of an allied counterattack. Two weeks later she attacked Iraqi shore defences, part of a diversion intended to make Saddam Hussein believe a naval invasion was imminent. The *Missouri*'s bombardment helped convince the Iraqis to keep their coastal divisions in place while the real offensive began in Western Iraq and Kuwait.

The Iraqis attempted to sink the *Missouri* by firing a Chinese-built HY-2 Silkworm missile at the battleship, but the Silkworm was intercepted by a Sea Dart missile fired by HMS *Gloucester* and crashed into the sea 700yds ahead of the *Missouri*. The *Missouri* remained in the Gulf until after the ceasefire.

On 7 December 1991 the *Missouri* was in Pearl Harbor to commemorate the 50th anniversary of the Japanese attack. The

ship decommissioned for the last time on 31 March 1992 at Long Beach, California, and she now serves as a floating museum at Pearl Harbor. The vessel that marked the end of the Second World War rests 500 yards from the sunken hulk of the USS *Arizona*, whose memorial commemorates the entry of the United States into the conflict.

The USS *Wisconsin* was again reactivated on 1 August 1986 and after modernisation was recommissioned on 22 October 1988, serving as a training ship and taking part in fleet exercises in the time leading up to the Gulf War. When operations began, USS *Wisconsin* was deployed with the *Missouri* to help protect Saudi Arabia as part of Operation Desert Shield. She fired Tomahawk Missiles against Iraq when Operation Desert Storm began. She remained in the Persian Gulf until after the ceasefire took effect in March 1991. USS *Wisconsin* was decommissioned for the last time on 30 September 1991, and she now serves as a museum ship at the Hampton Roads Naval Museum in Virginia.

Model Products

There is a huge number of kits available for this class of ship. There are several reasons for this:

- The popularity of the ships – they were the largest and best-looking American battleships.
- Their fame, and particularly the surrender ceremony on the *Missouri*

- Their long service life, coupled with the length of time that models of this class have been available.

The very first injection-moulded ship model to be released on the market was the *Missouri* made by Revell. This was first released in 1953 and is still available in 2011.

■ *IOWA* CLASS KITS

Scale	Company	Kit	Comments	Scale	Company	Kit	Comments
1:350	Tamiya	*Missouri*	1945 Configuration	1:700	Tamiya	*New Jersey*	1985 Configuration
1:350	Tamiya	*New Jersey*	1985 Configuration	1:700	Tamiya	*Iowa*	1943 Configuration
1:450	Hasegawa	*Missouri*	1945 Configuration	1:700	Trumpeter	*Iowa*	1985 Configuration
1:535	Revell	*Missouri*	First released in 1953	1:700	Trumpeter	*New Jersey*	1982 Configuration
1:600	Aurora	*Iowa*	OOP 1945 Configuration	1:700	Trumpeter	*Missouri*	1987 Configuration
1:600	Aurora	*New Jersey*	OOP 1945 Configuration	1:700	Trumpeter	*Wisconsin*	1988 Configuration
1:600	Aurora	*Missouri*	OOP 1945 Configuration	1:720	Revell (Germany)	*Iowa*	OOP 1945 Configuration
1:700	NNT	*New Jersey*	1985 Configuration	1:720	Revell (Germany)	*New Jersey*	OOP 1945 Configuration
1:700	Fujimi	*Iowa*	1945 Configuration	1:720	Revell (Germany)	*Missouri*	OOP 1945 Configuration
1:700	Fujimi	*Missouri*	1945 Configuration	1:720	Revell (Germany)	*Wisconsin*	OOP 1945 Configuration
1:700	Fujimi	*Wisconsin*	1945 Configuration	1:900	Nichimo	*Iowa*	1945 Configuration
1:700	Fujimi	*New Jersey*	1945 or 1968 Configuration	1:900	Nichimo	*New Jersey*	1945 Configuration
1:700	Tamiya	*Missouri*	1945 Configuration	1:900	Nichimo	*New Jersey*	Hypothetical Helicopter Carrier version

REVELL *MISSOURI*   1:535 Scale

This kit has been on the market for nearly 60 years. It was the first-ever plastic injection-moulded kit and it has an enduring popularity because of that. Initially released with magnificent box art by John Steele, this kit was to be found everywhere in the 1950s and '60s. The kit presents the ship as it would have looked at the end of the Second World War, and includes a plaque referring to the Japanese surrender signed onboard. There are two different versions of this kit: one with catapults and floatplanes, and one with helicopters and no catapults.

This is a decent model for kids just starting out, as it assembles easily. The kit itself was a good effort for its time but now it is severely limited. The hull is in one piece with an incorrect shape below the waterline. The hull is flat bottomed – it could be displayed on a shelf without a stand or for that matter pushed around the carpet without it tipping over. There are no propellers. The 20mm Oerlikons are all moulded on the decks and detail is poor overall.

Still, this model is a slice of history and as such would grace any collection.

Recent box art of Revell's 1:535 *Missouri* (not the classic work by John Steele).

AURORA *IOWA* CLASS (RELEASED AS *IOWA*, NEW JERSEY AND *MISSOURI*)

1:600 Scale

This kit depicts the *Iowa* class ships as they appeared in 1945. These kits were released in the early 1960s and were fair for their time. Their time has passed and they are generally sought for nostalgia reasons. Aurora has ceased to exist and for that reason many of its kits are considered rare and command high prices.

HASEGAWA *MISSOURI*

1:450 Scale

This kit was released in 1981 as one of Hasegawa's 'Famous Ships' series. This kit was designed to be motorised so the propeller and rudder details were sacrificed to this cause. The details are fairly basic and the casting is not the best. Three Curtiss SC-1 aircraft are included. This kit is scheduled to be re-released, presumably with improvements that reflect the substantial advances in the technology of injection moulding made in the interim.

TAMIYA *MISSOURI*

1:350 Scale

This kit was first released as part of Tamiya's original batch of 1:350 scale offerings. It was a vast improvement over all other kits on the market and became a mainstay for entries in model competitions. It was big, detailed and accurate. While an excellent kit for its time, it is beginning to show its age.

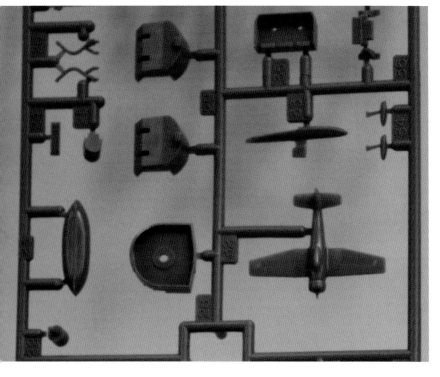

The kit scales out very closely with the actual dimensions: beam is right on and length is within .05in of the scaled measurement. The hull is moulded in a single piece up to the main deck. The waterline is scribed on the side to aid in either painting or waterlining the kit. The deck comes in three pieces, but the seams are limited to the short segments between the widest part of the superstructure and the deck edge. The planking effect is produced by raised lines rather than the recessed grooves seen in more recent releases, making hiding the small seams a bit more difficult. A partial dry-fitting of the kit shows that the pieces fit together fairly well, with only a minimal effort to hold the deck sections in place due to the tendency of such a large hull to warp inward. The 16in gun turrets are well formed with subtle detailing on the turret roof. Side detailing is limited by the two-piece moulds that were used. The guns are moulded as a single piece with the blast bags incorporated. This will allow only one position for the barrels. The 5in mounts come as three pieces: a main section and detailed side panels. Again, the barrels are designed for a single fixed position.

The superstructure detailing such as portholes, doors, ladders, piping etc is entirely missing on the lower deck levels. The only blemish on the pristine plastic is some moulded-on stairs – often referred to as Aztec stairs. This is odd since the upper levels and control tower have some detail. Perhaps the designers anticipated the wealth of after-market parts that would remedy this and save the modeller the trouble of sanding off the existing detail before applying after-market parts. Still, there are those Aztec stairways that need to be removed – not an easy task so perhaps some detail was warranted.

TAMIYA *NEW JERSEY*

1:350 Scale

■ This is essentially the same as the *Missouri* kit but has some different sprues to make this model represent the *New Jersey* as she appeared in 1985.

Like the guns, the Tomahawk box launchers are also moulded for a single fixed position. Some work will be required to reposition any of these components to other than the kit's static depiction. Most of the detail work is of a very high standard; the helicopters in particular are very nice. However, like the *Missouri* kit, there is a complete lack of detail on the superstructure sides on the two levels above the main deck.

One area that Tamiya failed to model correctly is the helicopter deck. On the actual ship, it is raised 10 to 12 inches above the main deck, with ramps at its forward end that lead down to the deck level. While this would be hard to notice in a smaller scale, 1:350 is large enough for this to stand out. The slightly elevated part of this deck should be easy to reproduce with a section of sheet plastic, but the tapered ramps will be a bit tougher to replicate.

Above: Note the detail on the helicopter fuselage.

Left: Note the almost total lack of detail in the main and upper deck superstructure bulkheads. The same shortcoming applies to the *Missouri* kit.

Below: This shows the sheer number of parts required to assemble this beautiful kit.

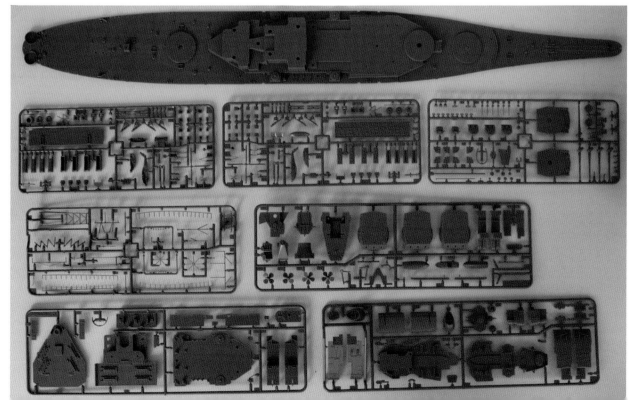

FUJIMI *IOWA* (ALSO RELEASED AS *MISSOURI* AND *WISCONSIN*)
1:700 Scale

SEA WAY MODEL アメリカ海軍 戦艦アイオワ U.S. NAVY BATTLESHIP **IOWA** **FUJIMI**

Below: This kit is the same as the other Fujimi kits of this class but has the extra sprue on the left to enable the modeller to build the kit to represent the *New Jersey* as she appeared in 1968.

This kit was released in the 1970s as part of the Waterline series. It was one of the better offerings in that series and was the first good quality model of this class. Dimensionally, it is quite accurate – the hull captures the sweep and sheer of the hull as well or better than any other kit. The superstructure, with the exception of the area just forward of the second funnel is largely accurate.

Like the Tamiya offering there is a complete lack of detailing on the first three levels of the superstructure – except the inevitable Aztec stairs. Released 25 years earlier than the Tamiya kit, the detail on the small parts is a bit cruder, but nonetheless satisfactory. A good model can be made from this kit, especially with the addition of after-market parts. It represents the *Iowa* as she appeared in 1945, after the bridge was remodelled along the lines of the *Wisconsin* and *Missouri*.

FUJIMI *NEW JERSEY*
1:700 Scale

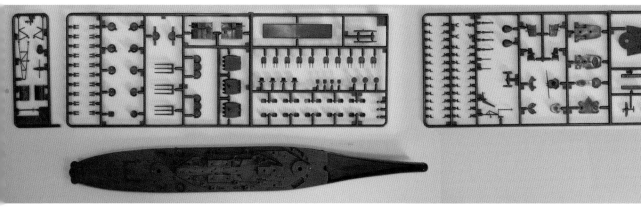

This kit is the same as the *Missouri* and *Iowa* kits with an additional sprue to allow construction of the *New Jersey* as she appeared in 1968 off Vietnam. It can also be built as the *New Jersey* as she appeared in 1945 after the bridge rebuild. Interestingly this is still the only kit on the market than can be built as a Vietnam era *New Jersey*.

SEA WAY MODEL アメリカ海軍 戦艦ニュージャージー U.S. NAVY BATTLESHIP **NEW JERSEY** **FUJIMI**

TAMIYA *MISSOURI*

1:700 Scale

The hull is waterline only, with the classic Tamiya base plate; no lower hull is included. The hull scales out extremely close to the correct dimensions, being about .09in short and .04in too narrow – hardly noticeable in this scale. The upper hull is moulded in two pieces, allowing more side detail than is available in their earlier 1:350 kit. Like the 1:350 release, the main deck is moulded in three pieces. The seams are similarly placed in the narrow strips between the superstructure and the hull sides. Unlike the earlier kit, the deck planking is depicted by recessed grooves, making it easier to fill and hide them. Because much of the planking was removed aft, the seams here are less of an issue.

Dry-fitting of the major parts shows a generally good fit overall. Many of the side bulkheads are included as separate pieces, allowing an improvement in the level of detail, but there are still sections lacking. Most notable are the long sections of the first level of superstructure where side detail is totally absent. Turret detail is limited to single lines of rivets and a few

moulded-on ladders. Turrets 2 and 3 have the usual rangefinders as separate pieces. The barrels are moulded with the blast bags attached, and so are limited to a standard fixed elevation without some effort on the part of the modeller. The 5in mounts are devoid of side detail and also have the fixed barrel positioning in common with the larger guns.

Despite its shortcomings, this kit is a significant improvement in detail over the 1:350 version and even a step up from Trumpeter's offering. Tamiya's typical accuracy also gives it an advantage over the competition and an excellent model can be made using this kit.

This shows the large number of parts included with this kit. Most of these sprues are to be found in the *New Jersey* and *Iowa* kits but each of these kits has some different sprues to customise the ship to its individual appearance at that time.

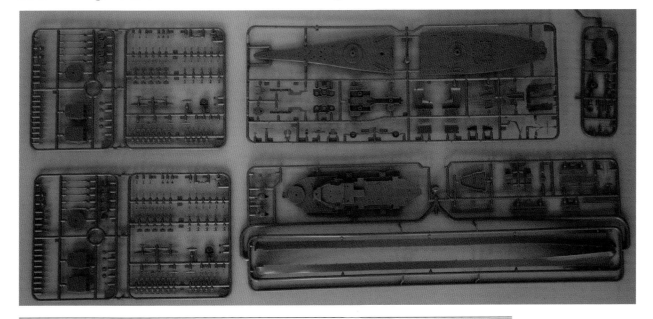

TAMIYA *IOWA*

1:700 Scale

The Tamiya *Iowa* shows the ship as she appeared on commissioning and before her first refit in 1945. Basically it is the same kit as the *Missouri* with a different sprue for the bridge and conning tower parts. These were notably different from her sisters after they were commissioned. This is the only kit in any scale that builds into a mid-war *Iowa*.

The instructions show a version of the camouflage which appeared in late 1944 but shows the colours as Haze Gray and Navy Blue. The box art reproduced here shows Dull Black and Haze Gray. Unfortunately, it does not have a diagram of the striking and unique feathered

camouflage that the *Iowa* wore in early 1944. Modellers will have to use pictures or other references to paint the model in this iconic scheme.

TAMIYA *NEW JERSEY*   1:700 Scale

The Tamiya 1:700 *New Jersey* is a more recent release than their 1:350 offering, and as such takes advantage of many of the improvements available in the newer kits. As in the 1:350 kit, the Tomahawk launchers are similarly limited

One can see the fineness of detail not only on the helicopters but also for the 16in turrets.

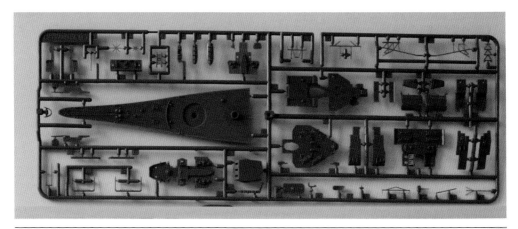

Note where the break in the deck falls – much of it is obscured by superstructure making the seam between deck pieces easier to disguise.

to a standard fixed position. Like the 1:350 kit, the helo deck is not raised above the main deck, but in this scale it is less noticeable. The helicopter itself is very nicely detailed as in the 1:350 version.

When it first appeared, the fact that the specific *New Jersey* parts were on a separate sprue raised hopes for the future release of the modernised sisters. This would have been similar to what was seen in the Tamiya *Missouri* and *Iowa* kits that were marketed at about the same time. However, the modernised sisters never materialised, perhaps because of the release of Trumpeter's series of modern *Iowa*s.

This makes it all the more frustrating that Tamiya chose not to proceed with the sister ships. What this kit lacks can be easily made up for with the after-market detailing sets, and when these are obtained, it can be built into an excellent model.

Note the lack of Aztec stairs and the inclusion of surface detail in the main deck bulkheads.

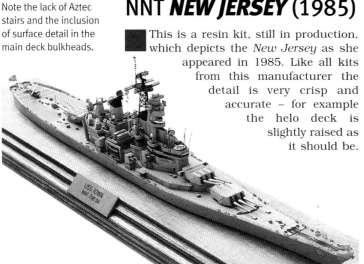

NNT *NEW JERSEY* (1985)   1:700 Scale

This is a resin kit, still in production, which depicts the *New Jersey* as she appeared in 1985. Like all kits from this manufacturer the detail is very crisp and accurate – for example the helo deck is slightly raised as it should be.

The small details are particularly nice. One that is especially well done is the main battery rangefinder atop the fore and aft control towers, which has the correct shape and thickness – all other models in this scale are deficient in this, which is a shame because it occupies such a prominent position on the model. The kit comes with photo-etch for the radars and other fine detailing. Good though this kit is, it would still benefit from the addition of some of the after-market sets – particularly 5in twins.

TRUMPETER *WISCONSIN* (1991) 1:700 Scale

The Trumpeter *Wisconsin* is a good quality kit recently produced by this prolific Chinese company. Filling a gap in the market, Trumpeter has released a series of four modernised *Iowa*s and has included the minor differences of each ship in the respective kits. The kits have all the same sprues with different decals and instructions.

The 'bones' of these kits are good; the hull shape is excellent and of the correct dimensions. A dry fit shows that the parts go together well. The detail is not as good as the Tamiya kits and the deck is a disappointment – the planks are delineated by raised lines and there are spaces as much as .8mm, which scales out to deck planks 560mm (22in) wide.

Like every other important plastic kit of this class of ships, it is devoid of bulkhead detail with the exception (of course) of the inevitable Aztec stairs.

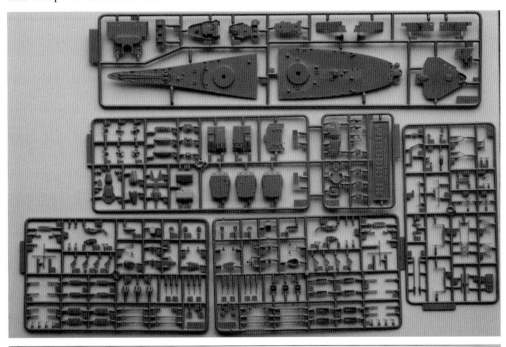

This set of sprues is the same for all of the Trumpeter modernised *Iowa* kits. There are parts for all the variants and the instructions and decals differ for each kit.

TRUMPETER *NEW JERSEY* (1982) 1:700 Scale

This kit contains the same sprues as the *Wisconsin* but does not use many of the parts as it represents the earliest incarnation of the modernised *Iowa* class.

For example, there are no radomes in front of the control tower and abaft the stack. Even though some compromises were made for production reasons, this is a reasonably accurate model of the *New* *Jersey* as she appeared in 1983 off Lebanon.

This kit was also released as an *Iowa* (1987) and as a *Missouri* (1988) with different instructions and decals.

This shows how the deck and superstructure forms part of the hull. The deck seam just forward of the aft turret will be difficult to hide.

REVELL *MISSOURI* (ALSO RELEASED AS *IOWA*, *WISCONSIN* AND *NEW JERSEY*)
1:720 Scale

These kits were released by Revell Germany in the early 1980s as part of their constant scale series. Why 1:720 was chosen for the 'constant scale' when 1:700 was firmly established is a mystery. They are out of production now but can be found on eBay or at kit auctions.

The hull is the best feature of this kit. It

is a three-piece hull, with port and starboard halves, plus a piece that fits between the twin skegs. The hull halves are not scored for waterlining, but considering how well it is done below the waterline, you will probably want to build it as a full-hull model anyway. Even the bulbous bow is right.

The detail parts are not as good as the hull. They cannot be easily replaced by the numerous 1:700 after-market sets because of the scale difference. Though it is small, it is enough to make the detail parts unusable – for example 1:700 40mm quads will not fit in the gun tubs.

This kit was good for its time but is not in the same league as the 1:700 kits now on the market.

Photo-Etch & Accessories
1:350 Detail Sets

There are some impressive and comprehensive sets available in this scale specifically designed for the Tamiya kit. Two Chinese firms, Flyhawk and Lion Roar, have produced comprehensive and very similar superdetailing sets with brass, resin and extensive photo-etch in 1:350 scale.

LION ROAR *MISSOURI* SUPERDETAIL SET   1:350 Scale

This superdetail set lives up to its name, consisting of 18 photo-etch sheets, 31 turned brass parts and 191 resin parts.

The photo-etch is very well done with a massive amount of detail. All of the detailless superstructure on the Tamiya *Missouri* can be covered by photo-etch sheets with portholes, ladders, doors and piping. The photo-etch sheets have open door spaces and separate door frames so they can be installed open or closed as one chooses. This will create a more realistic model in that these ships almost always had a mixture of doors open and secured. Many of the parts are very delicate and some assemblies are quite complicated, so this is not a set for the feint-hearted.

The instruction is a 30-page booklet showing parts use und assembly in three-coloured isometric drawings. The parts count in itself should be a warning: study the instructions and the kit closely. The detail set does not absolve you from studying references; it just supplies you with the maximum of choices for your superdetailed build of the USS *Missouri*.

Turned brass parts comprise nine 16in/50 guns, twenty 5in/38 guns and two beautifully done ship's bells. The resin parts consist of fourty-two twin 40mm Bofors, eighty ammo boxes, two anchors, nine 16in gun blast bags, twenty-five 5in/38 blast bags, with resin guns

attached, thirty gun directors and two practice guns. Some resin parts are wisely included as the plastic parts of the Tamiya set are inadequate (40mm barrels, and Mk 51 gun directors) and they need more dimension than PE is capable of (notable the 40mm twins and anchors). An interesting decision is to provide resin 5in guns with blast barrels and metal barrels without. If one wants to use metal barrels with blast bags then surgery is required. This is not absolutely essential as the *Missouri* is rarely pictured with blast bags on the 5in guns.

FLYHAWK *MISSOURI* SET
1:350 Scale

This is another superdetail set along the lines of the Lion Roar set. They have a similar approach but there are important differences. Like the Lion Roar set, Flyhawk's set has photo-etched brass, resin and turned brass. Flyhawk tends to use smaller frets than Lion Roar so the fact that there are 30 frets of PE in this set does not represent a quantitative difference between the Lion Roar and Flyhawk sets. This set includes bulkhead detail for the Tamiya *Missouri* of the highest standard. For example, the bridge windows even have wipers. The photo-etch covers the gamut of virtually every detail that could be considered missing or needing enhancement on the Tamiya kit. The bulkhead detail is a bit more three-dimensional than the Lion Roar offering – the ladders fold over the superstructure sides rather than being relief-etched, for instance. Coupled with the separate watertight doors, this makes for a more realistic appearance when one chooses to open the doors and hatches. The detail is quite impressive: each door has the hinges, clips and turn wheels etched into them.

Of course the usual photo-etch details are included, such as radars, cranes, catapults, ladders and railing but to these are added numerous tiny details such as 40mm ammunition racks especially fitted to the various gun tubs, supports and gratings. Items such as propellers (four- and five-bladed), AA guns (the 40mm Bofors quads are done entirely in photo-etch), anchors and 20mm AA are done in photo-etch and for this scale they may seem a bit two-dimensional. Many of the assemblies are delicate and complex, so skill and care are needed to achieve a satisfactory result.

You also get an extensive set of resin which replaces large and small vents, gas bottles, practice guns, Mk 51 directors, Mk 57 directors, paravanes, boat controller, crane controller, crane base, 5in gun turrets, radar base and various catapult details. The 5in turrets are very nicely done but require the pour bases to be removed. Surprisingly there are no resin blast bags for the 16in guns – but those supplied in the Tamiya kit would make a perfectly acceptable alternative.

GOLD MEDAL MODELS *MISSOURI* PHOTO-ETCH SET
1:350 Scale

This is a complementary set of two frets from GMM. One is a set of the normal range of PE accessories for battleships customised for the 1:350 Second World War

Iowa class kits on the market. It contains railings in several different styles (including upswept railing for the bow), ladders, catapults and cranes, as well as a complete set

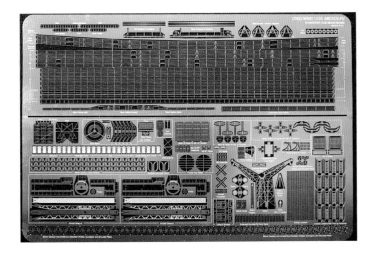
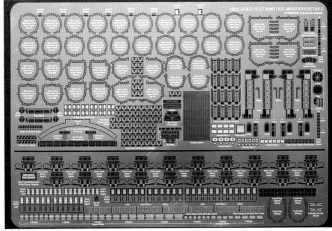

of all the radars and mast details needed for a 1945 *Missouri*. It also has bridge windows and assorted bulkhead details, such as watertight doors, lifebelts, etc. The additional set GMM 350-04a contains intricate superdetailing PE – notably for the 40mm quads. Ammunition racks and shields are provided for all twenty quads and their various shaped gun tubs. There are also additional ladders, doors and hatches, as well as platforms, stack detail and 3-D relief-etched oxygen and acetylene compressed gas bottles in racks for detailing bulkheads. Each of these sets is available separately.

WHITE ENSIGN MODELS *MISSOURI* PHOTO-ETCH SET
1:350 Scale

■ This set is similar to the GMM set described above in that it comprises two separately available frets which when combined make a superdetailing set for the *Missouri*. The primary set resembles the GMM offering in supplying cranes, cata-pults, boat davits and detail and especially shaped railings for the Tamiya kit. It also has a wealth of surface detail such as bulkhead doors and hatches. The secondary set has stack detailing, platforms, radars and floater-net baskets.

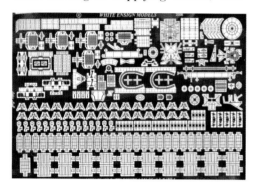
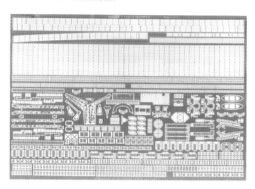

L'ARSENAL *MISSOURI* CORRECTIONS SET 1:350 Scale

Note the to scale 3-D anchor chain.

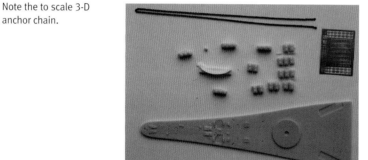

■ This set was specifically made to correct the minor inaccuracies on the bow of the Tamiya *Missouri* kit. There is also anchor chain and superdetailing for the capstans.

1:700 Detail Sets

A gain Lion Roar and Flyhawk lead the field in 1:700 after-market parts, as they do for 1:350, but there are also a few other interesting items on the market.

FLYHAWK *MISSOURI* SET
1:700 Scale

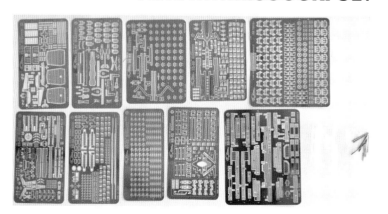

■ This is another superdetail set with ten photo-etch sheets and turned brass 16in barrels. In particular, it addresses the problem of the detail-less bulkheads on the 1:700 kits. It is designed for the Tamiya 1:700 *Missouri* kit but most of it can be used on the *Iowa* kit and – to a lesser extent – on the Tamiya *New Jersey* kit. It also can be used on the Fujimi and Trumpeter kits but some surgery is needed for a close fit (it fits the Tamiya kits like a glove). The fit on the Fujimi kit is quite good with the exception of the super-structure around the stack and the three

40mm gun tubs abreast the rear stack.

The rest of the photo-etch covers the usual items done in this medium: cranes, catapults, radars, mast details and, interestingly, the perforated plate under the anchor chain. There is no railing included so another after-market part such as the GMM superfine railing is needed.

The instructions are detailed and extensive but can be a bit hard to follow.

LION ROAR *MISSOURI* SET   1:700 Scale

■ The Lion Roar is very similar to the Flyhawk 1:700 set, being as extensive, accurate and excellent in its detailing. The range of components is also very similar. Like the Flyhawk set it has catapults, cranes, radars, mast details and railing They are not identical, however: the construction of bulkhead detail is different, as are items such as floater-nets, 20mm gun tubs and some radars. This set also has some PE 20mm twins, unlike the Flyhawk. Detailing on the bulkheads is excellent but the ladders are two-dimensional as opposed to the fold-over ladders on the Flyhawk set.

Both the Flyhawk and Lion Roar sets have complex 40mm quad structures with platform, trunnion and barrel assemblies and shield. These are intricate and delicate

assemblies so great care must be taken as there are no spares.

The instructions are comprehensive and easy to follow.

This shows the nine PE sheets and turned brass gun barrels. The PE frets are larger than the Flyhawk ones and railing is included.

LION ROAR 5in TWIN TURRETS   1:700 Scale

■ This set comes with resin turrets, brass barrels – with hollow muzzles – and PE ladders for twin 5in turrets as found in *Iowa* class battleships. They are superbly detailed and easy to assemble. The only possible drawback is that they come with blast bags moulded onto the turrets and if the modeller wishes to depict this set without blast bags (which was common practice on the *Iowa*s), major surgery is required.

NIKO 40mm QUADRUPLE MOUNTINGS   1:700 Scale

■ These are a combination of PE and resin which give a more 3-D feel to the Bofors. They are much more detailed than the plastic ones included in the kit and they are more robust and realistic than the PE ones included in the superdetail sets.

PAPERLAB 20mm GUNS

■ These are very finely cast in white metal. The detail and scale is more accurate that the various kits guns and they are more three-dimensional.

Modelmakers' Showcase

Virtually every ship modeller has at one time built a model of the USS *Missouri*. So too have the four modelmakers featured in this section, along with models of the modernised *New Jersey*.

These models are in four different scales – 1:96, 1:192, 1:350 and 1:700 – and they make an interesting comparison, showing the effect of scale on painting, detailing and presentation.

TAMIYA *MISSOURI* AND *NEW JERSEY* 1:700 Scale   By KOSTAS KATSEAS

Below: By all accounts the narrow bow made the *Iowa* class wet ships.

Bottom: Wallowing in heavy seas. Note the differences in colour between the running and standing rigging.

Right: This shows the level of detail one can achieve in as small a scale as 1:700.

Kostas Katseas, who is well known to people who frequent ship modelling websites, is a prolific professional modeller who works in 1:700 and 1:350 scales. Kostas hails from the small town of Drama in the mountainous region of northern Greece. This seems appropriate given the dramatic nature of his models. His interest in military modelling stems from his childhood exposure to war movies, which inspired him to replicate the onscreen images in three dimensions.

He started out putting together 1:72 Matchbox aircraft, but larger scales intro-

duced him to painting and superdetailing, which developed into a penchant for accuracy and a flair for colour and drama. Kostas then moved on to ship kits. His first effort was the 1:700 Matchbox *Bismarck*. He spent a year eyeing the kit and its wonderful box art before he could afford to lay his hands on it. It remains one of his favourites.

His reason for settling on ships was simply that he likes the shape of them: they are very elegant (well, most of them). That is the main factor, but size/scale is also important. For example, a small harbour diorama in 1:700 can depict a vast area with as much detail you can cram into it. In any other scale you would need an entire room and half a lifetime to build it.

Kostas then travelled to London to study computer systems and lived there for 15 years, studying, working (at all sorts of jobs from bicycle courier to chef) and, of course, building models – primarily ships in 1:700 and 1:350. Soon he began to meet people who were willing to pay him to build ship models for them. The appeal of getting paid for his hobby had him building almost 100

Top left: A good view of the scratch-built mast, Harpoon missile tubes and Tomahawk missile boxes juxtaposed against the old 5in/38 twins.

Above: A full view of the model and base.

Top right: This view captures the mood: a careworn *New Jersey* at anchor and resting after a lengthy mission in the Indian Ocean.

Right, middle: Details like the painting crew at work give the model a life and interest above and beyond the excellent craftsmanship evident in this model. The ship looks tired and rusty; it is at rest and the crew have set about cleaning it up. Note the plate seams and how they add to the overall look of the model.

Right: Although much of this model is built from kit sets and accessory packages, certain things had to be scratch-built for accuracy and dimensional correctness. The mast is an example of this.

per cent of the time for other people. In 2009 he returned to his home town and took this exercise to a new level. He is now building even bigger, more dramatic, more complex and expensive models on commission for people around the world.

Both models featured here were commissioned for overseas clients. The *Missouri* was made using the Tamiya *Missouri* kit, adding resin 5in turrets and Flyhawk superdetailing set. It is now in Melbourne Australia. The *New Jersey* is also made from the Tamiya *New Jersey* kit, with the addition of the GMM photo-etch set and Lion Roar 5in gun turrets. A lot of small

details were added, such as an entire new mast. Kostas tried to created a visually more interesting hull by scribing some of the plate seams along the hull using Tamiya masking tape as a guide. After he sprayed the hull colour, he simply dragged the knife along lightly. After a few oil washes, all the detail came to light. The *New Jersey* is now in Tokyo.

To enhance the look of the deck Kostas sprayed a base colour very lightly, and then picked up individual planks with a fine brush with various tones of the base colour. Once dry, he applied a few oil washes of brown and raw sienna.

SCRATCH-BUILT *MISSOURI* 1:350 Scale

By PIERRE MARCHAL

Pierre Marchal is an outstanding modeller who lives in Paris. He has been interested in warships and ship modelling since childhood when a diet of movies about the Pacific war inspired a lifelong interest in the US Navy. At the time he lived in Africa – this was in the 1950s – so he was isolated

from hobby shops and had to improvise. Developing techniques taught to him in a high school woodwork class, Pierre used wood and the drawings from *Jane's Fighting Ships* to construct scratch-built models of his favourite US ships in the 1:1530 scale of the drawings in *Jane's*. He taught himself

other scratch-building methods so that he was not restricted to building whatever models were available as commercial kits; he could build whatever he was interested in – and all in the same scale. Pierre has never built a plastic model.

His modelling activities lapsed during university studies, marriage and starting a career. Pierre worked in the petrochemical industry and has travelled extensively worldwide. He ended up as the manager of a jewellery company based in Spain before he finally retired in 2007. During his career he never lost interest in ship modelling and at 35 he started again with a more satisfying scale of 1:500. Pierre kept on devel-

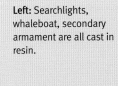

Above: A good model can tell a story. In this case we see that the Japanese surrender party has just arrived and the dignitaries are assembling just abreast No 2 turret.

Left: Searchlights, whaleboat, secondary armament are all cast in resin.

Above: A wealth of detail – and all scratch-built.

Below: Much of the fine detail in this picture comes from photo-etch specially designed by Pierre. He designed the support structure for the Mk 34 gun directors abreast the forward stack.

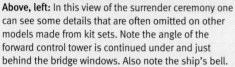

Above, left: In this view of the surrender ceremony one can see some details that are often omitted on other models made from kit sets. Note the angle of the forward control tower is continued under and just behind the bridge windows. Also note the ship's bell.

Above, right: A close-up showing the table and Japanese party.

Right: Using differing thicknesses and colours makes the rigging look very realistic. The very fine thread used is true to scale in 1:350.

Below: The Japanese surrender party faces the green table where MacArthur and the other allied representatives await them.

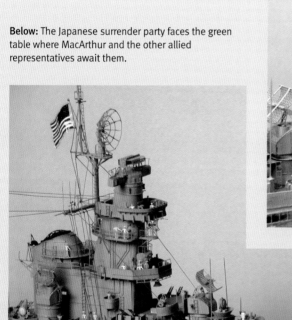

Right: Pierre used aluminium tubes to make the 16in barrels. The turrets are made of wood. Splinter shields and other fine detail is made from paper.

oping his scratch-building skills and in 1:500 there were lots of drawings available from the Ships' Data source. But 1:500 was still a bit small and in 1995, after a visit to the United States, Pierre settled on 1:350 as his scale of choice. The *Missouri* pictured here was made three years later in 1:350 scale and was entered in Naviga 2000 where it won a gold medal. He modelled the *Missouri* as she appeared at the surrender ceremony. In addition to using detailed plans, Pierre referred heavily to the many photos taken on that day. He placed rather less crewmen than there were in the pictures so as to not over-clutter the model while still giving a representational feel to the project.

Pierre has developed some unique modelling techniques to achieve the effects he requires. He uses paper where other builders use styrene; paper is thinner and

more to scale. In this beautiful model Pierre used paper to make the cranes, details on vertical parts such doors and hatches and splinter shields. Pierre also makes lots of his own photo-etch. The gunsights, platforms and other fine details on the 40mm mounts are an example of this, as are the 20mm.

In building this model of the *Missouri* as she appeared after her final refit in 1945, the principal parts of the ship including hull, superstructure and turrets are all made of poplar wood. For rigging Pierre uses thread for making flies for fishing (made in Canada). He uses two colours, brown and black, for effect. The standing rigging is black and the signal halyards are brown. The water is made with acrylic painting mixed with a gel to give it a luminous effect. When the 'sea' is dry he airbrushes with 'micro satin' to give the sea its sheen.

Below: This gives a good view of the aircraft crane and catapults which were made from a combination of wood, paper and photo-etch

SCRATCH-BUILT *NEW JERSEY* 1:192 Scale
By JOSEPH NEUMEYER

Below: Port bow view.

Bottom: Blast off – someone should tell the captain not to launch too close to the shore.

This exciting 1:192 (1/16in = 1ft) scale model was constructed by Joseph Neumeyer of Dynamic Dioramas. It is not the *New Jersey* as we know it – rather a visualisation of possible *Iowa* class power in the future.

The diorama was commissioned by Ted Yadlowsky of the United States Naval Fire Support Association and the concept was strongly endorsed by the US Marine Corps. The diorama was sent to Washington DC, and was on display for a year in a secure briefing room in the Rayburn Building, within the Capitol complex. This was to encourage interest within the defence establishment in the usefulness of a third modernisation of the *Iowa* class as a fire support vessel for the Marines. This one

is of the *New Jersey* as she would have looked in 2003 after a third modernisation and refurbishment. It is escorted by two Mark V Special Forces attack boats.

Joseph has been interested in modelling – especially dioramas – since he was a youngster in Hancock Park. As a teenager he would recreate land battle scenes; after carefully building models of the tanks, figures and artillery he would stage 'live action', complete with firecrackers, gasoline and other dangerous effects. While Joseph may not have been the only teenager to do this, he is one of the few who has managed to make a career out of it. Although Joseph

no longer ignites his dioramas, they are still very dramatic and exciting.

Although there is plentiful information on *Iowa* class battleships, for this model Joseph had to improvise a design using ordinance that would suit the new role. The secondary weapon (replacing the twin 5in) is the new 5in/62 Mk 45 Mod 4 gun. This is the new standard USN 5in gun, as used on the new Flight IIA *Burke* class destroyers. He upgraded the Harpoon missile tubes to a more advanced version, and in place of the Phalanx is the 30mm Goalkeeper CIWS, standard on NATO ships for the last 20 years, and the Mk 38 Mod 2 'Bushmaster'

Above: The illusion dispelled – the model on its base.

Below: The beautifully sculpted missile contrail is highlighted by the small electric light hidden in the translucent tube which the contrail is built around. This view also affords a close look at the Harpoon missiles, Bushmaster and CIWS system.

Above: This starboard quarter view emphasises the large size of the MV-22 Osprey on the fantail.

Right: The starboard bow of this fast moving warship. Note the speeding Mark 5 patrol boats.

Below: Close-up view of the bridge, a mix of the Second World War and the twenty-first century.

Left: This gives a good close-up of the deck. The wooden deck was fabricated from a sheet of fine strips of hardwood. The strips were approximately 1/16in in width, all of which were attached to each other with a thin strip of black adhesive tape. Joseph applied a sanding sealer to the sheet and sanded it smooth, cutting the sheet into various shapes to match the many decks and deck fittings located throughout the ship.

Above: A good view of the lovely MV-22 Osprey, a tilt-rotor aircraft designed for expeditionary assault, raid operations and special warfare – operationally perfect for the *New Jersey*'s new mission.

Left: The Osprey positioned on the helo deck.

Right: Ship's boats: note the realistic weathering and rust patterns on the *New Jersey*'s hull.

Below: In reality, this would be dangerously close to the speeding behemoth.

Bottom: This crane is used to replenish other ships in the task force – this ability to carry extra fuel and stores was a major reason to reactivate these ships.

25mm chain machine gun system – it is mostly for keeping away the smaller surface intruders The *piece de resistance* is the VLS system installed just forward of the aft control tower. This model is shown firing a Standard Missile (SM-3), but can launch any number of different kinds of missiles.

The hull of this model was a standard fibreglass *Iowa* hull from Scale Shipyard of Long Beach California. They also supplied the turret guns and other standard fittings such as cable reels and missile tubes. These basic fittings were considerably enhanced by scratch-building extra detail. For instance, the missile tubes had various rods, cylinders, training wheels and other detail added to the basic forms. The missile launch contrail and smoke was sculpted using a hybrid mixture of materials, including cyanoacrylate glue around a translucent acrylic tube containing and concealing electrical wires for the light used to simulate the fire of the rocket exhaust.

Other components were taken from other kits and modified to suit. Often the part would bear no relationship to what it was used for in the *New Jersey* but it had a similar shape or complexity to what was needed.

There are many rewards to modelling but one of the most unusual compliments that Joseph has received was relayed to him by one of the US Navy missile personnel in the Weapons Department stationed at Naval Base Venture County. When shown high-detail photos of the missile launch, they actually thought they were looking at the real thing. One officer remarked, 'At sea, we never launch so close to buildings on shore,' to which the response was: 'That's not a building! It's a front-porch railing.' To this the somewhat surprised and amazed officer replied in jest: 'That's either the largest front-porch railing I've ever seen, or the smallest battleship!'

SCRATCH-BUILT *MISSOURI* 1:192 Scale

By JOSEPH NEUMEYER

About ten years previously Joseph built a 1:192 scale model of the *Missouri* as she appeared in 1945. This was displayed in a Los Angeles model shop that Joseph had an association with.

Left: A full model view of the *Missouri*. This model is over 4ft long; it served as a dress rehearsal for the *New Jersey*.

Left: Amidships view of the *Missouri* as she appeared in late 1945. Dockyard clean and crisp.

Left: This shows the beautiful deck detail that Joseph includes on all of his ship models

SCRATCH-BUILT *MISSOURI* 1:96 Scale

By JOHN R HAYNES

Below: At this scale (1:96) the tiniest details can be fabricated. Note the shape of the railing stanchions and the droop of the chain between the stanchions just abaft the stack.

Bottom: The full model, which is over 9ft long.

This 1:96 (1/8in = 1ft) scale model of the *Missouri* enjoys an iconic status that cannot be matched – it resides in the ward-room of the ship it represents.

John Haynes is a professional model-maker who lives in Essex, England. He has been producing models as a career since 1978, but he did not start out to be a modelmaker – in fact he did not start making models until he was an adult. As a youngster he was fascinated with Meccano sets, and anything mechanical sparked his interest. His father served in the Royal Navy in the Second World War, on the *Hood*, (prior to May 1941), the *Warspite* and later

with Walker's famous hunter-killer escort group. John had always loved ships and as an avid Meccano enthusiast developed the dexterity for what was to become his life-time career.

Johns trained as an engineer and had every prospect of a successful career in that field, but naval interests – sparked by his father's career and hours of gazing at all the beautiful ship models in the nearby Imperial War Museum – led him into making a model out of balsa wood, ply and brass. A fortuitous meeting with Dr Jonathon Steinberg lead to a visit to the Bundesarchiv in Freiburg Germany and

Left: A good look at the aircraft crane and Seahawk scout planes. The 40mm quads are made from a kit devised by John and is available through John's online shop.

allowed John access to detailed plans of the *Scharnhorst* – one of John's favourite ships. He spent three years on this model, working after hours and on weekends, and making up techniques as he went (John is entirely self taught). The *Scharnhorst* model was seen by people from the War Museum and they were so impressed that John was offered a job restoring the models that he had gazed at when he was a youngster. This was the fork in the road for John, but for him the choice was easy – he resigned as an engineer and has been building and restoring models ever since.

He now builds about three models a year

– mainly for private collectors in America as well as museums and other organisations around the world. His virtually flawless models are generally made to order in 1:96 or 1:192 scale. They are all scratch-built but John produces common parts for ships en masse for use in other models. They are available through his website www.john-rhaynes.com/shop/index.php.

The model shown here now resides in the wardroom of the *Missouri* herself, which gives extra kudos to the excellence and accuracy of the model. It took John about a year to build, to a commission in 2002 for Steve Maguire of Maguire Industries who

Below: The *Missouri* in John's well-equipped workshop.

Above: The raison d'etre of this battleship: 16in/50 rifles. Note the attention to detail, like the windscreen wipers on the bridge windows.

Below: This shows the relatively uncluttered quarterdeck and lovely hull lines of this class.

subsequently donated it to the museum ship *Missouri*.

The hull is made of fibreglass and the superstructure is fabricated from wood faced by aluminium. Weaponry such as Bofors and 20mm guns are made to order by professional casters using John's patterns and then assembled by John himself. For example, each quad mount consists of cast resin trunnion with metal accessories, The main battery consists of cast resin turrets and turned brass barrels. The main deck is 2mm ply over the deck beams. For rigging John uses crochet cotton and other threads such as medical suture used for stitching wounds. John developed his own photo-etch for catapults, cranes, radars, platforms, and other fine detailing. If these items are of general usefulness they may end up in John's online shop.

Illustrations by George Richardson

Iowa as completed 1943

In Measure MS 22. The horizontal surfaces were Deck Blue

CAMOUFLAGE - MEASURE MS 22

5 - L
LIGHT GRAY

5 - N
NAVY BLUE

20 - B
DECK BLUE

Iowa late in 1944

In Measure MS 32, Design 1B. The dark colour is uncertain and may be Dull Black. The horizontal surfaces were Deck Blue

CAMOUFLAGE - MEASURE MS32a / 1b

5 - L
LIGHT GRAY

5 - N
NAVY BLUE

20 - B
DECK BLUE

Missouri as completed June 1944

In Measure MS 32, Design 22D. Designed for destroyers, the horizontal surfaces were Deck Blue (20-B) except for the lighter areas of the pattern, which were Ocean Gray (5-0). This scheme was replaced by Measure 22 before the ship went to the Pacific in November.

CAMOUFLAGE - MEASURE MS 32 / 22D

5 - O
OCEAN GRAY

5 - L
LIGHT GRAY

20 - B
DECK BLUE

DULL BLACK

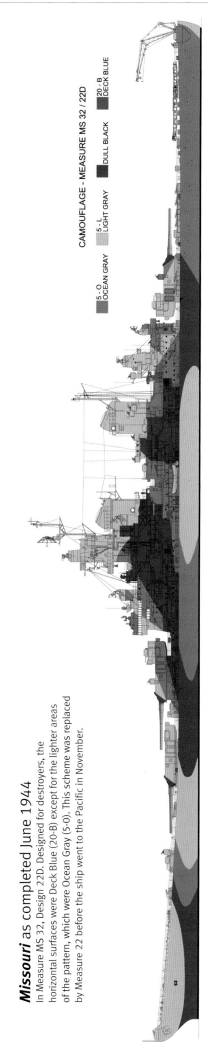

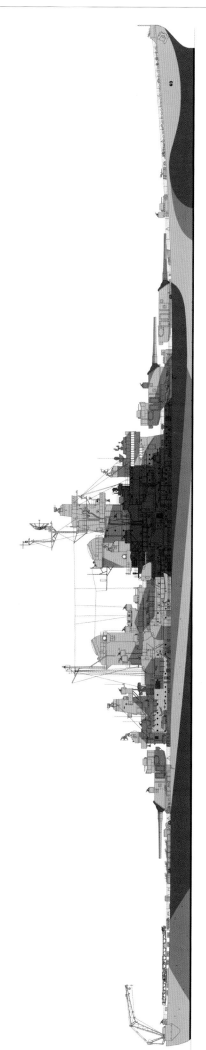

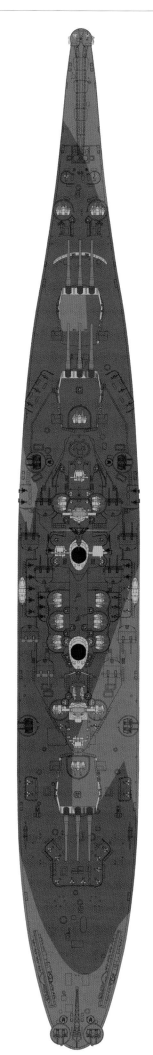

Illustrations by George Richardson

A view of the *New Jersey*'s portside 5in 38-calibre secondary armament, and quadruple 40mm mounts. Note the large arcs of fire available to both weapon types.

Iowa 1986: The new look – clean lines, no mainmast, large lattice foremast, no crane on the fantail and mix of the old and new in the weaponry. For all that, the lines of the ship are the same as they were in 1943.

A view of the two major weapon systems of the 1980s in action – 16in guns and Tomahawk cruise missiles.

The *Wisconsin* after her final refit. One can see the Tomahawk missile boxes amidships, the Harpoon launchers abeam the aft stack and the CIWS weapons. Even with these changes and the addition of massive radar and other electronic masts and arrays the ships profile is unmistakeably that of an *Iowa* class battleship.

Appearance

The *Iowa* class battleships are considered by many to be the most beautiful warships ever built. They have very graceful lines and a fine balance. There is a long majestic sheer line forward flattening out just before the superstructure rises above it. This was followed by a tall control tower and then two evenly spaced stacks, the lesser aft control tower with a generous quarterdeck beyond that. The balance was exquisite – the turrets seem perfectly spaced, the control tower just the right height, and the proportion and spacing of the funnels just about ideal. Over the years and many refits and modernisations the basic look has remained unaltered. They are instantly recognisable as *Iowa* class battleships. For over half a century the *Iowa*s have represented the image of all battleships.

Like many beautiful ladies, however, they look better from certain angles and there are some vantage points which do not flatter. The hull shape was unique with a very fine bow that narrowed in plan view. From certain angles it looked odd – like a long thin proboscis jutting forward from the massive hull. The control tower was similarly slender; although it looks in proportion when viewed from abeam, seen from the bow it looks a bit skinny.

Throughout their long service lives the four *Iowa*s were very similar in general appearance – but not always at the same

time. When one ship would go in for a refit she would often emerge with features introduced earlier on her sisters and then maybe have an additional modification.

The *Iowa* as completed was relatively unadorned compared to her sisters. Because she was fitted out as a flagship, there was an extra level in the conning tower for the flag officers. To keep their view unobscured, No 2 turret only had 20mm Oerlikons mounted on top unlike the bulkier 40mm quad mounted on all three of her sisters. Around the conning tower there was an open walkway. Her AA fit in 1943 had only fifteen 40mm quads, but before she was sent to the Pacific in 1944 she had four more quads added – two abreast the aft turret, each replacing a pair of 20mm, and two on the bow, just where it narrows

The initial bridge configuration of the *Iowa*. The conning tower has a walkway around it. Note the simple foremast stepped back from the fire control tower. Note also the slits on the conning tower ahead of the walkway where the admiral's position was. This would have been obscured had the No 2 turret mounted a 40mm quad instead of the three single 20mm. Also note the Mk 3 radar atop the conning tower and SG radar on the platform high up in the fire control tower.

Iowa dressed overall, 12 June 1957.

bringing the total to 20 quadruple mountings. Other than these features and her camouflage pattern, the *Iowa* and *New Jersey* were remarkably similar in 1944.

Next to arrive on the scene was the *Wisconsin*, which was very similar to the *New Jersey* and *Iowa* except for the area around the conning tower. A roomy square-fronted enclosed bridge was built around it. This square bridge became the standard and was installed in all of the *Iowa*s by 1945 and this distinctive and prominent feature remained with this class for the rest of their service lives.

The foremast was different in that it had a platform for the SK air search radar and a pole on the after part of the platform for the SG radar – this had been mounted on a platform in front of the fire control tower in the *Iowa* and *New Jersey*. The *Wisconsin*'s mainmast was originally the same as the one on the *Iowa* and *New Jersey* but just prior to her arrival in the Pacific it was strengthened and extended and an SP air search radar was mounted on top. The Mk 3 radar on the conning tower of the *Iowa* and *New Jersey* was replaced by a small Mk 27 ranging radar.

The *Iowa* sailed home for a refit and returned in May 1945 looking very much like the *Wisconsin*. When the *Iowa* went stateside she was replaced by the *Missouri*, which was almost identical in appearance except for the prominent SK-2 air search radar mounted on the foremast platform. It was a large bowl-shaped radar instead of the flat SK set on the other ships. Also the ship did not have the heightened mainmast and SP radar that the *Wisconsin* did. Otherwise the *Missouri* was configured much the same as the *Wisconsin*.

In April 1945, after a refit, the *Iowa* returned to the Pacific fleet. The ship had been remodelled with a square bridge like the *Missouri* and *Wisconsin*, painted in the same camouflage scheme (Measure 22) and fitted with a platform on her foremast. She did retain her flat SK radar (configured as in the *Wisconsin*) and her three 20mm Oerlikons on No 2 turret.

When the *Iowa* arrived, the *New Jersey* left for a long overdue refit, which was

Above: From this angle the long thin prow and skinny control tower are very apparent.

Below, left: The round bridge configuration initially installed on the *New Jersey*.

Below, right: The square bridge fitted to the *Missouri* and *Wisconsin*. This configuration was later fitted to the *Iowa* and *New Jersey* during their refits in 1945.

forward of turret No 1, replacing a trio of 20mm.

With regard to radar, the *Iowa* was fitted with SK air detection radar atop the foremast, SG radar located atop the mainmast and on a platform high up in the control tower. For fire control they had Mark 8 radars atop the big rangefinders on the fire control towers and a Mark 3 ranging radar atop the conning tower.

The *New Jersey* followed the *Iowa* out of the shipyard with a few changes: the walkway around the conning tower was closed in. The *New Jersey* (and her later sisters) did not require visibility from all levels of the conning tower so an extra quad 40mm was added to the top of No 2 turret,

Above: *Iowa* in the Pacific in January 1944. Note unusual feathered camouflage scheme

Below: The *Iowa* in June 1944 with the feathered areas filled in. She could be said to be wearing Ms 32/1B completed.

completed in July 1945 – with all the usual modifications such as square bridge, platform on mainmast, SK-2 radar, plus a new feature – her mainmast was strengthened and stepped back from the aft stack. The *New Jersey* was on her way back to the combat zone when the war ended. Her bombardment of Wake Island en route to rejoin the fleet was said to be the last battleship rounds fired in the Second World War.

CAMOUFLAGE SCHEMES

By the end of the Second World War all the *Iowa*s wore the same camouflage, but prior to that the ships had carried a variety of camouflage schemes. The *Iowa* herself had the widest variety of patterns. When first commissioned and operating in the Atlantic the *Iowa* wore Measure 22 – Navy Blue (5-N) hull up to the deck amidships and a straight line extending fore and aft from there, and then Haze Gray (light grey, 5-L) above that (the sheer of bow and stern, and the superstructure).

By the time the *Iowa* went to the Pacific, however, she was painted in Measure 32/1B. This was an exotic splinter camouflage using only two colours: Haze Gray and Dull Black (or possibly Navy Blue; it is not absolutely certain). In early 1944 she appeared in a unique feathered scheme with hard edges and feathered edges to the camouflage. She was well known for this unique look. By June 1944 there was no more feathering – hard edges only. It would appear that the feathered areas had been filled in. There is no mention of a change in camouflage measure in the historical

record. Perhaps the 'feathered' camouflage could be better described as 'incomplete camouflage'.

The *New Jersey* was much less ambiguous. After a brief stretch in the Atlantic where she wore Measure 22, she arrived in the Pacific in Ms 21 – Navy Blue on all vertical surfaces and Haze Gray on all horizontal surfaces.

The *Missouri* bucked the trend. Whereas the *Iowa* and *New Jersey* were commissioned in the relatively conservative Ms 22 schemes and then reverted to more dramatic schemes when in the combat zones, the *Missouri* was commissioned wearing the very flamboyant Measure 32/22D camouflage scheme, originally a design for destroyers but adapted for an *Iowa* class BB.

Sadly, this was all painted over in Measure 22 before the *Missouri* shipped out for the Pacific. The kamikaze threat negated all the splinter camouflage schemes such as 32/22D and virtually all ships active in the Pacific were painted in Measure 22 (or Ms 21) by 1945. This included the *Wisconsin* and refitted *Iowa* and *New Jersey*.

POSTWAR AND KOREA

After the war, the ships were all painted Haze Gray (5-H) and the decks holystoned to a natural teak colour. The stacks and mainmast were painted black and the ship's number was enlarged and given a drop shadow for better visibility. This paint scheme was retained for the Korean War and after. In the age of radar the need for visual concealment was considered unnecessary.

Opposite, top:
Starboard view of *Iowa* in December 1944 entering ABSD-2, the floating dry dock at Ulithi. She is still in Ms 32/1B completed.

Opposite, middle:
When commissioned the *Missouri* wore Measure 32/22D, a scheme originally designed for destroyers. Unfortunately for modelmakers, it was painted over before she joined the Fifth Fleet.

Opposite, bottom:
Portside view of *Missouri*'s fancy camouflage

After her 1945 refit *New Jersey*'s mainmast was stepped aft of the second stack. This was done in all the other *Iowa*s by 1954.

BB62
Broad on Stbd. Quarter

Above: The crew of the *Missouri* assembled on the anniversary of the surrender of Japan, August 1949.

Below: *Iowa* in April 1952, showing the typical appearance of the class during the Korean War. Except for minor differences in radar all the ships looked very similar. Note the lack of catapults and the position of the aircraft crane. The stepped mainmast and foremast configuration are also plainly visible.

By the time the Korean War erupted, the *Missouri* and *Iowa* had stepped mainmasts similar to the *New Jersey*. The *Wisconsin* had hers added during a refit. The catapults aft were removed and helicopters were used instead of floatplanes. The crane was retained for handling purposes but typically it was pointed aft – over the fantail so as to not impede helicopter operations.

During the Korean War all the *Iowa*s were very similar in appearance – much like the *New Jersey* appeared in 1945. However, there were some minor changes to the 1945 look. On Mk 37 5in directors Mk 4 radars were replaced by the similar Mk 12/22 then in turn replaced by the round dish of Mk 25 in 1952. The *New Jersey*, *Iowa* and *Wisconsin* were fitted with SPS-6 air search radar while the *Missouri* retained SR-3. After the war the *Wisconsin* upgraded to SPS-12.

In 1955 the *Wisconsin* had an SPS-8 height-finder fitted to her mainmast. To carry this the mainmast required strengthening. The *Iowa* had large kingposts for ease of handling refuelling operations added as an integral part of the mast strengthening. *Wisconsin* followed suit in 1955.

By now the *Iowa*s were being put into reserve and, other than hermetically sealing all the remaining AA armament, no further changes to their appearance were made until 1968 when the *New Jersey* was recommissioned.

VIETNAM ERA

The *New Jersey* was recommissioned and given an 'austere' refit, in which much more was removed from the ship than was added. All of the light AA armament was stripped off as well as most of the splinter shields. Four 40mm gun tubs were retained, painted white and were used as swimming pools by the crew. However, several very visible items were added that substantially affected her appearance. On the bow a large monopole radio antenna was mounted just forward of where the two 40mm quads were previously situated. The fire control tower had a huge (and hideous) box mounted on it to house an electronic countermeasures

Left: A view of the mast details of the *New Jersey* during her Vietnam stint.

Below: *Wisconsin* in 1957: note the kingposts supporting the refuelling booms and doing double duty supporting the mainmast, with the SPS-8 on the platform. Also observe the ever more complex foremast configuration – three platforms, three masts. Atop the main battery rangefinder is the new Mk 13 fire control radar.

Above: The large monopole antenna mounted on the bow of the *New Jersey*.

Below: The newly refurbished *New Jersey* on her way to Vietnam in June 1968. Note the radio mast on the bow – mounted just forward of the where the two 40mm gun tubs used to be. Also note the complete lack of AA guns.

system. (ECM) This was meant to confuse enemy radar and RF homing.

The masts were again changed to house a bewildering variety of radars, radomes, communications systems and electronic equipment such as radar jammers and direction-finders. The foremast was enlarged and sprouted several new platforms to support this equipment and the mainmast had some supports and yardarms added. Unlike the *Wisconsin* and *Iowa*, there were no kingposts used in supporting the mainmast. Amidships four Zuni chaff launchers were installed in the now vacant 40mm gun tubs between the two stacks.

Despite all of these alterations there was no mistaking the *New Jersey* for anything other than an *Iowa* class battleship.

THE 1980s

When the ships were recommissioned for what was probably the last time during the 1980s, they were rebuilt to a relatively uniform look. After decades of making the mainmast more elaborate and complex, it was removed entirely. The mainmast was gone, but the foremast was now a huge lattice capable of supporting whatever new radars and electronic gadgets were deemed necessary for modern warfare. New weapons were added, old ones removed. The Haze Gray paint scheme that they wore since 1945 was retained.

The *New Jersey* was the first one recommissioned and as such she retained the square ECM box on her fire control tower. It was pruned of the various antenna arrays that bristled outwards like whiskers on a

cat and seemed to fit better aesthetically because of this. The three other ships had a more elegant structure in the same place that looked like it belonged there in the first place. The massive lattice mast that did support all of the radars and antenna arrays seemed to complement the fire control tower and the battleship's silhouette regained its former grace and balance.

Four 5in twin turrets were removed to make room for the new armament. Harpoon missile launchers were mounted abreast the after stack where the three 40mm gun tubs used to be. On either side of the Harpoons, platforms were built to support the armoured box launcher for the Tomahawk cruise missiles. A large deckhouse was constructed between the stacks to house missile guidance systems, on top

of which were mounted two Phalanx CIWS systems. A sophisticated boat handling system was installed underneath the forward Tomahawk platform.

The most interesting of all the new fittings was a specialised refuelling boom on the starboard side just forward of the No 3 turret. The *Iowa*s had been used for re-fuelling and replenishment on an ad hoc basis for the previous 40 years, but the installation of this boom made it official – the *Iowa*s were multi-purpose ships with tanker and storeship capability.

The lattice mast was the most prominent feature of the rebuilt *Iowa*s. It replaced the multi-platformed affair that had evolved over the years and took on much of the equipment previously mounted on the mainmast. The lattice mast was stepped right over the

In 1968 *New Jersey* had a large ugly box added to the fire control tower to house the electronic jamming equipment and provide a mounting for the large ULQ-6 electronic counter-measures system. The Mk 25 dish radars installed on the secondary gun directors are still there.

forward stack. It was essentially a tripod mast with lattice supports for strength which culminated in a huge platform above and just behind the fire control tower. This platform supported its primary radar array consisting of an SPS-49 air search radar, an SPS-67 surface search radar, some ECM equipment and a pole topmast which was covered in electronic arrays.

Aft was a slightly raised helicopter platform but the aircraft crane was removed. Much of the teak planking on the quarterdeck was covered in a protective surface for helicopter operations.

This configuration was used for all four *Iowa*s and there were very few differences between them. The *New Jersey* retained her square box ECM structure where the other three had a more elegant seven-sided structure in the same location. The *Missouri* and *Wisconsin* sprouted large radomes late in their career. There were differences in the application of non-slip surfaces on the quarterdeck – but all in all, they were as alike as they ever had been.

Above, left: A good detail view of the *Iowa*'s fire control tower as it appeared in 1987. Note the more graceful shape of the ECM structure located above the Phalanx CIWS system.

Above, right: The new ECM structure is clear in this October 1986 view of *Missouri*.

Below, left: Harpoon missile launchers aboard the *Iowa*, October 1985.

Below, right: The *Wisconsin* preparing for the recommissioning ceremony in October 1988.

Above: A midships view of the *Missouri* in October 1991 showing most of the new features: the lattice mast above the forward stack, Tomahawks, Harpoons, Phalanx weapons systems and the fancy boats and davits. Note the large radomes on the aft stack and just below the ECM structure on the fire control tower.

Below: Less cluttered but essentially the same: *Iowa* in November 1984 (bottom) compared with *Wisconsin* in September 1944.

A close-up of the refuelling boom on the *Wisconsin*, August 1988.

A good view of the lattice mast on the *Missouri* in October 1986. The SPS-49 is clearly visible and just below it is the SPS-67 solid state set. The mast seems less cluttered than previous arrangements except for the shish-kebab of electronic arrays on the pole topmast rising from the platform.

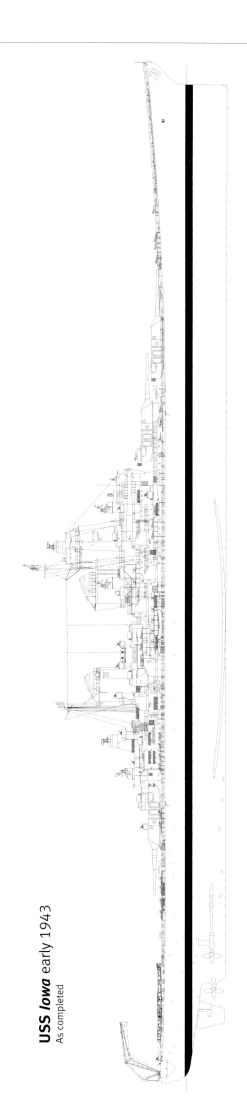

USS *Iowa* early 1943
As completed

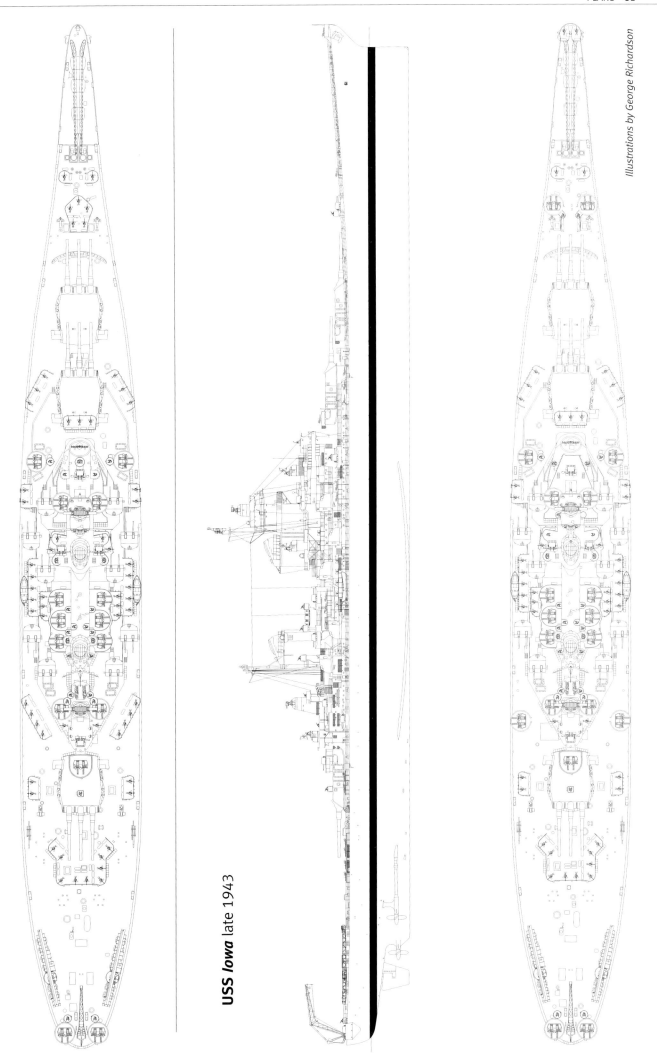

USS *Iowa* late 1943

Illustrations by George Richardson

USS *Missouri* 1944

USS *Wisconsin* 1956

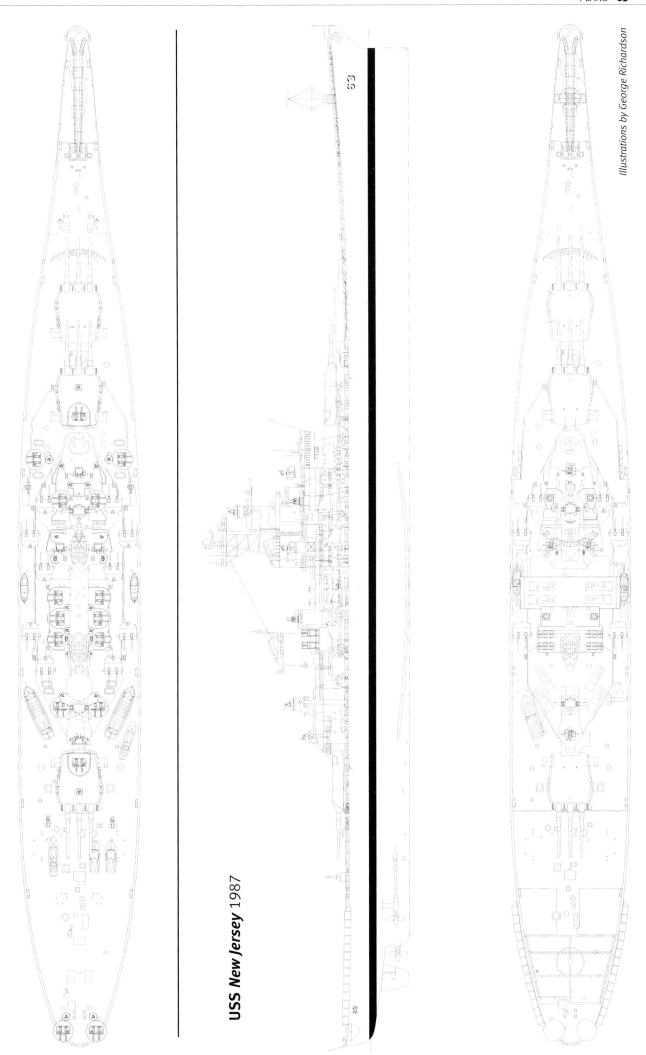

USS *New Jersey* 1987

Illustrations by George Richardson

Selected References

Friedman, Norman, US *Battleships: an Illustrated Design History*, Naval Institute Press, Annapolis 1985

Morison, Samuel Eliot, *History of US Naval Operations in WWII:* Vols *VII Aleutians, Gilberts and Marshalls; VIII New Guinea and the Marianas; XII Leyte; XIII Liberation of the Philippines; XIV Victory in the Pacific; XV Supplement and General Index*, Little Brown and Co, Boston 1951, 1960

Muir, Malcolm, *Iowa Class Battleships*, Blandford Press, London 1987

Preston, Antony, *Battleships*, Bison Books, London 1988

Stern, Robert *US Navy 1942 – 1943*, Arms and Armour Press, London 1990

Sumrall, Robert, *Iowa Class Battleships*, Conway Maritime Press, London 1988

US Navy Vessels 1943, Naval Institute Press and Arms and Armour Press, Annapolis and London 1986. Originally published in 1943 as ONI 54 series.

Walkowiak, Thomas & Sowinski, Larry, *United States Navy Camouflage of the*

WW 2 Era Part 1, The Floating Drydock, Philadelphia 1976, 1988

Wiper, Steve, *Warship Pictorial 16: USS New Jersey BB-62*, Classic Warships Publications, Tucson 2002

WARSHIP MODELLING WEBSITES

www.Dynamicdioramas.com
www.ipmsusa.com
www.johnrhaynes.com
www.modelwarships.com
www.smmlonline.com
www.steelnavy.com
www.warshipmodelsunderway.com

WARSHIP RESEARCH WEBSITES – *IOWA* CLASS

www.shipcamouflage.com/
   warship_camouflage.htm
www.navsource.org
www.history.navy.mil
www.classicwarships.com
www.hazegray.org

ACKNOWLEDGEMENTS

Steve Wiper   Joseph Neumeyer
Richard Jenson   Mark Jenson
Elizabeth Abbey

Iowa in Boston Harbor on 27 August 1943. After grounding during her work-up period, the ship was repaired and prepared for operations to screen Russia-bound convoys from the threat from the *Tirpitz*.

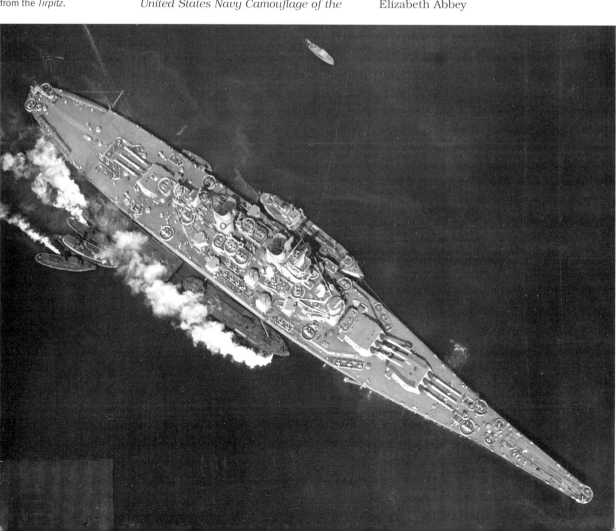